FOR SUCH A TIME AS THIS

AN EMERGENCY DEVOTIONAL

HANNA REICHEL

WILLIAM B. EERDMANS PUBLISHING COMPANY
GRAND RAPIDS, MICHIGAN

Wm. B. Eerdmans Publishing Co.
2006 44th Street SE, Grand Rapids, MI 49508
www.eerdmans.com

Published 2025
Printed in the United States of America

31 30 29 28 27 26 9 10 11 12

ISBN 978-0-8028-8592-0

Library of Congress Cataloging-in-Publication Data

A catalog record for this book is available from the Library of Congress.

"This is the book I have been waiting for. Every page, every sentence imparts uncommon wisdom for such a time as this. Sparingly written yet conveying remarkable historical and theological depth, this is a book every Christian should read and reread, now and in the days ahead. An invaluable gift to the twenty-first-century church."

—**KRISTIN KOBES DU MEZ,** author of *Jesus and John Wayne: How White Evangelicals Corrupted a Faith and Fractured a Nation*

"To live in perilous times, we all need perspective and inspiration, and Hanna Reichel offers both. *For Such a Time as This* is like taking a daily vitamin for our soul—every page is filled with good things to make us stronger. If we all read one entry a day and take its message to heart, together we'll become the change we long to see in our world."

—**MARIANN EDGAR BUDDE,** bishop of the Episcopal Diocese of Washington, author of *How We Learn to Be Brave: Decisive Moments in Life and Faith*

"In times of tumult, I am often drawn to quiet, daily rhythms to help ground me. That's why I'm thankful for Hanna Reichel's *For Such a Time as This*, a devotional primed to help us keep calm when all seems like crisis. Both specific and universal, history lesson and mystical meditation, each entry is immediately relevant to our current context yet also echoes with ancient wisdom. In an era that screams for outward action, this small book draws us inward and upward to reorient and nurture our souls and refresh us for the work of righteousness."

—**JEMAR TISBY,** author of *The Color of Compromise: The Truth About the American Church's Complicity in Racism*

"Hanna Reichel has written the book many of us have been looking for: a devotional guide for addressing the challenges and tragedies of our times. Insightful, wise, and powerful, this is a must read for American clergy, individuals, academics, and congregations."

—**VICTORIA J. BARNETT,** general editor of the Dietrich Bonhoeffer Works in English series

"In any crisis it's helpful to remember how faithful witnesses from the past navigated the crises of their time. But the art of interpreting the past for the present isn't simple work. It takes care and discernment. *For Such a Time as This* reveals Hanna Reichel to be a master of the craft. This book reads like a classic for the present."

—**JONATHAN WILSON-HARTGROVE,** author of *Revolution of Values: Reclaiming Public Faith for the Common Good*

"In these pages, Reichel makes a compelling case to pay attention. This is a task of love and resistance, of hope and protest, of dreaming and remembering, of creating space and taking space. For those drawn to such a life-affirming call, this book is for you."

—**AMAR D. PETERMAN,** author of *Becoming Neighbors: The Common Good Made Local*

To those who taught me what Christian witness looks like:

Gretel, Marie, Jorge, Dirkie

To those who will have to carry it forward:

Janita, Joshua, Junia, Ariella Rose

Contents

Part 2

"Hear the Word," *or* Listening and Responding

Part 3

"Become What You Have Received," *or* Communion

Part 4

"Go into the World," *or* Sending

How to Read This Book

You can read the short chapters of this book as stand-alone lessons, meditations even. The "First Aid Kit" on page 137 directs you to individual themes and the chapters that treat them.

You can also read the chapters in sequence, as an interconnected course of study. Four parts of seven lessons each, plus introduction and conclusion, would give you a daily prompt over the course of a month.

You may read this book on your own, or with a group. The "Study Guide" on page 139 offers reflection questions, action prompts, and resources for further reading.

The book's four parts—or weeks—are arranged according to the liturgical order of a worship service: gathering, listening and responding, communion, and sending. So it is with this book: Part 1 allows you to arrive, reflect, and refocus. Once you have worked through your feelings and made space for discernment, part 2 invites you to listen and respond, offering affirmation and challenge, instruction and cautions. Part 3 grounds you in the communion, worship, and core practices of Christian life. Freshly equipped, you are sent out again by part 4 into wider circles of solidarity and resistance, into uncertain as well as hopeful futures.

"We've been here before" applies not only to the diagnosis but also to the resources. There is nothing new in the individual lessons or the trajectory as a whole: They present the very foundational assumptions and practices of Christian faith, refracted through the light of this particular situation, illuminated by this particular cloud of witnesses. But maybe, presented in this way, old practices will appear in a new light and offer a renewed promise.

The voices and illustrations are primarily those of Christians in the mid-twentieth century who resisted National Socialist ideology and politics out of their religious convictions. I draw on these voices not because they are canonical figures or flawless moral exemplars, not because they are uniquely authoritative or the most radical and faithful voices out there. They are not.

They are simply what I have to offer to the current moment, based on my biographical background and my scholarly area of expertise—the contribution *I* can make to the table around which we are gathering. We will need many different sources of wisdom, experience, and insight in this conversation. I hope you bring yours as well.

What I observe from where I stand is only part of the picture. What is called for in one situation might be a disaster in another.

You will even find that some of the lessons stand in tension with one another, sometimes forming complementing pairs, sometimes taking the same idea into a different, or even opposing, direction. There are no unequivocal beliefs, incontestable conclusions, or cure-all recipes. I am not asking you to agree with what I say and go apply it. I am inviting you to reflect and ponder, put into perspective and complement.

Resolving all tensions is a hallmark of ideology. Easy answers and clear-cut solutions are what authoritarianism offers. Part of the task upon us today is to resist these lures.

We must build up tolerance for complexity. We must train our capacity to hold things in tension. We must exercise our communal ability for nuance and contestation. Everywhere, discernment will be needed. Only so can we do justice to reality and to one another.

Introduction

"There Is Nothing New Under the Sun," *or* We've Been Here Before

As a scholar, I have closely studied this nation. It prided itself in its influence in the world, its intellectual leadership, its technological innovation, its economic prowess. But as global orders shifted, its social and political system, built for simpler times, crumbled. Political and economic crises damaged trust in the government. Polarization increased and made coalition building ever less feasible. Widening gaps led to social unrest, economic instability, and even violence in the streets.

The nation was overwhelmed and disoriented. Betrayal by political opponents explained any defeats. Perceived humiliation turned into resentment, feeding a desire to "be great again." Political rhetoric shifted into ever more belligerent registers as enemies abroad and minorities at home were scapegoated. A muscular strength was projected out of swagger, false claims, and ever more overblown claims to greatness. Special leaders—claiming for themselves special powers—rode waves of public disgruntlement against immigrants, intellectuals, and those visibly "other." Democratic processes were manipulated, checks and balances hollowed out. Executive overreach became the order of the day.

The nation I am talking about is Germany; the time is roughly a century ago. But maybe my description sounded familiar to you today. Maybe, like me, you find yourself thinking: We have been here before.

"There is nothing new under the sun," echo the words of the Teacher in my head, the anonymous figure of Ecclesiastes who is characterized as a wise man and previous king of Jerusalem (1:9). We have been here before. This insight creates disbelief, frustration, weariness, maybe even despair. But it does not mean that all efforts are in vain. It means that there is wisdom to be drawn from those who have gone through such times before. It means we are not alone.

I wrote my first book on Karl Barth, a Reformed theologian from Switzerland who lived and taught in Germany during the demise of the Weimar Republic and the Nazi rise to power. Barth was one of the early voices cautioning against the emerging political theologies of greatness and purity, of nationalism and militarism, and he became a leading voice in the Confessing Church, the portion of the German Protestant churches who resisted integration into the Nazi state.

My study focused on how Barth read inherited confessions of faith to ground his own confessing stance. Grounding himself in tradition gave Barth some distance from the turbulence around him and freedom to speak back to it with force and authority. For Barth, *doing theology* was itself a kind of public witness: As an intellectual and communal practice of reflection that responds to God's word, theology has a word to offer to its own time, formed and informed by the wisdom of earlier times.

In these past years, comparisons between the United States and the Weimar Republic have become commonplace in political analysis. As democratic institutions crumble, even literal Nazi salutes have reentered the public square. Shock and disbelief have given way to eerie feelings of familiarity, throwbacks to histories against which I had been raised to insist, *Never again*.

We've been here before. You won't like what happens next.

For some time, many of us hoped that this wasn't that, that we'd avoided the worst, that our democracy was still going strong. After all, that occasionally platforms or personalities might get elected (and unelected again) whom some of us find objectionable is, in fact, the sign of a healthy democracy.

But that hope grew thin. Polarization continued to increase to the point of people living in entirely different realities. Democratic elections were not conceded when they produced the "wrong"—and therefore unacceptable—results. Standoffs between different branches of government replaced checks and balances. A complete overhaul of the government and the legal, economic, and social order was readied, so that a candidate could hit the ground running who had openly declared that he would rule as "dictator on day one."

He has since made good on this, as well as many other of his scarier campaign promises, ushering in a politics of "shock and awe."

We can quibble about terms and definitions. Is what we're witnessing a rise of *authoritarianism*—where a strong leadership wields ever greater power with few institutional checks and little accountability to the public, while individuals can enjoy freedom and private life as long as they don't challenge the rulers? Is it emerging *totalitarianism*—where the state seeks to control every aspect of life, facilitated by propaganda, surveillance, and personality cult? Is it more aptly called *oligarchy*, *kleptocracy*, *plutocracy*, or *kakistocracy*, as the few, the wealthy, the selfish govern while degrading public decorum, political culture, and communal flourishing? When does it become justifiable to use the term *fascism*—which adds ideologies of national supremacy and militarism to the mix, as it directs violence both inward and outward to purify and expand the nation?

We can quibble about the merit of any individual policy implemented since. That is not my point. My point is the change of order from a functioning constitutional democracy to . . . *something else*.

I am not arguing that history is repeating itself. Every context is different, and we do well to attend to the complexity of our world today. But noting certain similarities directs us to models we could learn from. Those who had to navigate the breakdown of a democratic order and the rise of a fascist regime in another time and place might have some wisdom to offer us today.

As I studied the Confessing Church, the part of the German churches in the Third Reich who resisted Hitler's "alignment" politics, I have often asked myself: When has the moment come to stand up and publicly and prophetically declare what faith in Jesus Christ means and commands today? It might be that this moment is here. What should the church's response be?

At the same time, I have also increasingly come to appreciate the less dramatic and more mundane, less corporate and more individual, less exceptional and simply ongoing task of faithful living as the world around is rapidly transforming: the task of *doing* all our life and work *as confession*—as a response to God that, even so, responds with a different kind of resolve to the world around us.

This second task is just as important as the first. Maybe even more: After all, only some of us have the necessary time and platform to proclaim *the* faith of *the* church, or even the bandwidth to write the kind of forceful manifestos that might—now, or in some future—become *something like* a confession of the church.

But all of us must keep living despite what feels like the end of a world. And this task requires just as much discernment, just as much attention, and just as much resourcing.

This, then, is the task this little book sets for itself. It is meant for regular people who—regardless of our position on this or that policy that a current government may be advancing, and regardless of our vocation and standing in life—feel uneasy about the rising authoritarian tendencies.

People who are looking for some insight as to how to live as Christians in such a time as this. The lessons are particularly for those among us who are not necessarily looking to die a hero, but who are concerned about how to keep on living as followers of Christ.

"For everything there is a season," knows the Teacher,

> a time to break down and a time to build up;
> a time to weep and a time to laugh;
> a time to mourn and a time to dance;
> a time to throw stones away and a time to gather
> stones together.
>
> (Eccles. 3:1, 3–5)

What is needed first is discernment and orientation.
What times are these?
What are they calling for?
What tasks do they put before us?
Where should we look for wisdom?

PART 1

"PREPARE YOURSELF," OR GATHERING

1

"He Then Rebuked the Wind . . . ," *or* Find Calm

Many things will happen at once. It will feel like a storm: an onslaught of terrifying developments, an interminable bombardment with threats from all sides, a nauseating cascade of news.

Mark tells the story of Jesus in the storm: "A great windstorm arose, and the waves beat into the boat, so that the boat was already being swamped. But he was in the stern, asleep on the cushion, and they woke him up and said to him, 'Teacher, do you not care that we are perishing?' And waking up, he rebuked the wind and said to the sea, 'Be silent! Be still!' Then the wind ceased, and there was a dead calm" (4:37–39).

It is not easy to stay calm in the storm. But it is necessary. Physical flooding will sweep you away as you're frantically trying to keep your head above water or cling to something. Emotional flooding will immobilize you in the face of what overwhelms. Both responses are understandable, but they work against you.

Don't let the storm control your emotions.

Don't let the storm direct your response.

This storm is not a natural catastrophe. It is an intentional strategy. It is meant to shock and awe, to overwhelm and debilitate, to create panic and scatter energy. The projection of unstoppable power will be self-fulfilling if you let it.

Don't let it.

Worship and obedience are not the only ways to empower evil. Evil draws power from attention. Evil draws power from fear.

Don't give it more power.

Lot's wife's turning around to behold the devastation was enough to permanently immobilize her. Don't ignore or sugarcoat what is happening. But don't let it mesmerize you. Don't let it take your eyes off the road.

In his prison camp, Dietrich Bonhoeffer mused:

> I often notice hereabouts how few people there are who can harbor many different things at the same time. When bombers come, they are nothing but fear itself; when there is something good to eat, nothing but greed itself; when they fail to get what they want, they become desperate; if something succeeds, that's all they'll see. . . . Everything, whether objective or subjective, disintegrates into fragments. Christianity, on the other hand, puts us into many different dimensions of life at the same time. . . . We weep with those who weep at the same time as we rejoice with those

> who rejoice. We fear—(I've just been interrupted again by the siren, so I'm sitting outdoors enjoying the sun)—for our lives, but at the same time we must think thoughts that are more important to us than our lives.[1]

The storm is not an illusion; its dangers are real. Even so, it is also a distraction. No one can pay attention to all the things all the time. The highest waves raise your alarms—and may hide more inconspicuous but forceful blows. The waves may or may not crush you, but focusing on them will keep you from attending to what matters most to you. Karl Barth advises, "a short, sharp glance suffices."[2]

Don't let the storm steal your focus.

No one can live in a constant state of emergency. Energy and attention are limited goods. When the absurd and atrocious become the everyday, two things happen: First, people desensitize. We run out of outrage. What would have created a panic yesterday elicits only a frown today.

Second, the craving for normalcy is so strong that people will tolerate, even demand, exceptional measures. Unbridled decision making without regard for process or legal constraints will feel like a relief rather than a threat.

Not strong enough to govern by majority and process, Hitler ruled by emergency decrees, which he gave out in rapid succession. An arson attack on the German parliament in January 1933 became his ticket to remove all checks on his powers: Dealing with the emergency demanded emergency powers. Within eighteen months, Hitler had abolished all remaining democratic institutions, "aligned" all organizations of civil life, withdrawn from the League of Nations, created the gestapo, and started purging the civil service of Jewish employees. Finally, he took out by assassination all remaining opposition in the ranks of his own party in the so-called Night of the Long Knives in June 1934.

Creating a state of emergency is a political strategy to gain unrestrained power. Don't fall for it.

At the height of the tumultuous integration of the German regional churches into a centralized *Reichskirche*, Karl Barth wrote a landmark essay titled "Theological Existence Today." Today, he asserted, the task was "to do theology, and nothing but theology, as if nothing had happened."[3] This demand raised eyebrows, then as much as now. Surely indifference is not the right response to the dismantling of civic life and democratic institutions?

But Barth neither advocated for indifference nor did he practice it. He played an important role in the Confessing Church, which declared the Hitler-devout German Christians a heresy and created their own parallel structures in resistance to Nazi co-optation. Barth lost his position, was prohibited from publishing and public speaking, and was forced to leave the country. From Switzerland, he would soon urge other nations that fighting against Hitler meant to fight "for the church of Jesus Christ."[4] Aged fifty-four, he even volunteered to serve in the Swiss reserve forces. And the essay itself did not advocate for indifference but engaged with different factions in his church, finding all of them theologically lacking in their resistance to the forced integration.

But Barth understood something that might be worth remembering today: Totalitarianism is about total control. It wants to control not just the public but also the private spaces. Not just politics and economics and education and religion, but also your thoughts and feelings. It does not need your love; your fear is enough.

Keeping your focus, feelings, and thoughts your own is hard. But it is itself an act of resistance.

Be strategic with your attention.

Knowing that a storm is brewing will allow you to be prepared. Losing sight of the horizon under crashing waves won't. Checking your social media feed every hour will not help you. Having spaces and times free from it will.

Follow the news, but limit your exposure. Ask yourself: Am I gaining important information, or am I giving away my attention? Am I focusing on what matters, or am I just getting dizzy?

Keeping some areas of life from the all-extending grasp is hard. But it generates spaces where other thoughts can be thought, other feelings can be felt, other priorities can reign than those dictated by emergencies real or staged.

If there is to be a life beyond totalitarianism, we must cultivate a life outside its grasp, even as we live within it.

2

"And Jesus Wept," *or* Feel Your Feelings

When Jesus learned of the death of his beloved friend Lazarus, what follows in John's gospel is—with two words and only nine letters in English—the shortest verse of the Bible: "Jesus wept" (11:35 KJV).

Jesus wept. Full stop. This is enough to fill a verse. Jesus let himself be deeply moved, and he sat with his grief rather than moving on.

Emotions impact your body, your mind, and your will. Feel them before you express them, think them, or act on them.

Feelings are responses to how the world affects you. Being affected can be uncomfortable. It can be overwhelming and scary. It alerts us to the fact that we are vulnerable, finite, and dependent on others. Because we like to limit our vulnerability, we tend to limit, avoid, or repress the feelings it causes. But doing so makes us no less vulnerable, it only makes us numb and brittle.

Reinhold Niebuhr was Dietrich Bonhoeffer's teacher at

Union Theological Seminary and influenced not only US politics but also the Confessing Church. He wrote the famous serenity prayer:

> God, grant me the serenity to accept the things I
> cannot change,
> the courage to change the things I can,
> and the wisdom to know the difference.[1]

The serenity prayer is one response to feeling overwhelmed and having limited agency, and it is a prudent one. It is the prayer of the Christian realist who preserves mental and emotional energy for the more effective causes.

The Christian idealist, on the other hand, might pray a slightly different prayer. I learned it from Argentinian singer-songwriters León Gieco and Mercedes Sosa, who, in defiance of a regime that copied the Nazis' technique of "disappearing" thousands of political dissidents, sang:

> Sólo le pido a Dios
> que lo injusto no me sea indiferente
> que la reseca muerte no me encuentre
> vacía y sola sin haber hecho lo suficiente.
>
> The only thing I ask of God
> is that I may never become indifferent to injustice
> that arid death may not find me
> empty and alone, without having done enough.[2]

One of the greatest dangers in times of mounting crises is desensitization. Exposure to violence leads to normalization of violence. If too many things are out of your control, it is tempting to numb yourself, to become indifferent, so as not to have to feel the discomfort and scariness of your lack of control and agency.

It is no exaggeration to say that our humanity is at stake in preserving our ability to feel.

Viktor Frankl, a psychiatrist and Holocaust survivor, chronicled the intense depersonification that affected prisoners of concentration camps. Even after liberation, they were so numb that they were unable to experience pleasure, beauty, and joy. On their journey to regain feeling, it was their bodies that brought them back into life. Cravings for food and for rest would assert themselves first.[3]

Emotional numbing is a trauma response. It protects you from pain, panic, and breakdown. It allows you to endure the unspeakable by shutting it out, by locking it away.

But it does nothing to mitigate the dangers your feelings flag. Nor does it preserve your ability to care for another moment. In fact, it erodes your capacity for empathy. It isolates and detaches you, deprives you of joy and hope, and eventually erodes your will to live. The damage lingers long after the danger has passed.

The only thing I ask of God, León Gieco repeats verse for verse, is to not become indifferent—to pain, to suffering, to war, to betrayal, to the future.

Emotions do not work according to an economics of

efficiency. They expand your ability to bear the world, and to transform it.

Empathy is a muscle. Strengthen it.

Allow yourself to be affected by the world around you.

Allow yourself to sit with the discomfort and scariness of being affected.

Give yourself permission to feel your feelings. Doing so requires time and space; it requires attention and some care.

Feel your body. It is beautifully designed and does most of its work unnoticed. Don't only pay attention to it when it breaks down. Feel the air expanding your lungs, the sun and wind on your skin, the earth underneath your feet. The whole universe conspires to support your every breath and step.

Care for your body to care for your soul. Note the sensations in your body. Note how your body responds to them in its own underground language. These responses may be externally prompted, but they are *your* responses. They are part of your agency rather than your exposure. They are also signals from your system to remind you about who you are, what you value, what you hope and fear.

Anchor yourself in your body, but also find ways to zoom out from where you are to preserve your ability to feel. If needed, create contrast artificially. Watch movies and read books from other times and places. Let art give reality back to you in a starker light. Remember and record changes in the world and your response to them. Compare notes with others. Offer your feelings to God and let God bless and transform them. Listen to music that will whip up a storm in your soul.

Conserving your emotional energies for "realistic" hopes will only dry them up. Feel all the feelings. Pour out your emotions and let them create rivers in the landscape.

Lazarus had been dead for four days. If Jesus hadn't wept for him, how could he have brought him back to life?

Many die every day without resurrection hope. Don't deprive them of your tears or of your righteous indignation. The driest earth only needs a few drops.

3

"Deprive Them of Their Pathos," *or* Test Your Feelings

Feel all your feelings, but don't just trust them.

Emotions are not just personal; they play a powerful role in shaping political life. Name them, question them, and reflect on them before you act on them.

Political emotions fuel civic engagement and democratic movements. Indignation over injustice, corruption, and abuses of power can be a motivator for protest and change. Hope in making a difference and shaping the future feeds grassroots participation. Trust in other people and institutions is necessary for the division of labor that turns passion into social change.

There are no bad feelings. But unprocessed feelings can easily turn into desires, thoughts, and actions that you might want to check. Raw feeling can easily be leveraged by ideologues and propagandists who want you to follow passionately rather than critically, and to act on impulse rather than discernment.

The political and economic instability of the Weimar Republic came with a volatile emotional mix. As the fledgling democracy staggered under the impact of enormous reparation payments and the Great Depression, as millions experienced poverty, unemployment, and social degradation, feelings of fear and humiliation, hopelessness and desperation, resentment and rage spread widely.

The Nazis were extremely skilled in harnessing these emotions. At mass rallies they converted individual anger into collective rage. They stoked nostalgia and offered a sense of belonging, destiny and purpose, catharsis and meaning. They directed negative feelings away from the government and against the democratic system. They built up love for and loyalty to the leader while channeling anger against Jews and Marxists, intellectuals and "traitorous" elites, ethnic minorities and foreign powers, disabled and queer life.

The Nazis used disgust and contempt to undermine political discourse and foster violence against political opponents. Fear and anger fueled their vision of renewal and redemption, pride and prosperity, unity and awe.

Many of these promises were false; others were horrific in their concretions. But the appeal to emotional needs of security and revenge, pride and belonging was extremely effective: They paved the way for authoritarianism, destroyed democracy, and inspired an ideologically united nation to violently purge itself of its "impurities" and fight against its "enemies."

There is a lot of space for all kinds of emotions in the Bible, but time and again it insists: "Do not be afraid." Fear is one of the most easily abused emotions. Authoritarian regimes leverage, curate, or even carefully build up senses of existential threat, real or imagined. Widespread fear allows them to consolidate power, suppress opposing viewpoints, expand surveillance, and unify people ideologically.

Feelings of anxiety and worry can easily be channeled into resentment and envy, scapegoating immigrants, political dissidents, or supposed "enemies of the state." Fear narrows love and moral responsibility. Those with whom one identifies—the family, the nation, the state, often the leader himself—will get played out against other objects of love and devotion. Difference turns into a sense of threat. When curiosity and empathy give way to disgust and contempt, violence is not far.

In his Romans commentary, Karl Barth grappled with the danger of political emotions, too. Even the response of outrage against the situation, he saw lucidly, can spiral anxiety further. An arms race between different politics of emotion will only feed the fear and urgency that strengthen ideology. To undermine this, it will be more effective to abstain from fanning the flames: "Deprive them of their pathos, and they will be starved out; but stir up revolution against them, and their pathos is provided fresh fodder."[1]

When feelings fuel politics with pathos, examine your emotional responses. Untested emotions only feed the beast. Depriving politics of pathos is a way to minimize its ability to turn fear into hatred, passion into uncritical thought, urgency into violence, and violence into counterviolence. Depriving politics of pathos is a way to starve ideology. Testing your emotions gives you some critical distance over the way things affect you and allows you to harness them for your own purposes.

As you give yourself permission to feel all your feelings,

also give yourself permission to develop a relationship with them. Ask them about their places of origin and the journey on which they want to take you.

Feelings are symptoms and indicators; their messages require active discernment and translation. Ask yourself, what does this feeling reveal about the world? What does this feeling reveal about who you are, what you care about, and what takes you off guard?

Some feelings disguise themselves as other feelings: Which part of this grief is guilt? How much of your outrage is envy? Is your anger just thinly veiled helplessness?

Some feelings disguise themselves as thoughts and opinions: Is your envy really a judgment about your neighbor's life or one about yours? What is this feeling to you, and why?

Some feelings lend themselves easily to certain actions, but most give you options: Fear can translate into freeze, fight, flight, or fawn. Disgust can inspire withdrawal or attack. Anger can be channeled into rage and violence, or into indignation and solidarity.

Ask yourself: What is it you want to do *because* of this feeling?

Then ask yourself: What do you want to do *with* this feeling?

Let your feelings, all the feelings, build your capacity for self-reflection, empathy, and discernment.

4

"Test the Spirits," *or* Practice Discernment

There is a reason the Bible talks about the devil as "the antichrist." Evil likes to pose as salvation, and to harness the power of faith for its falsified gospel. There are clear and overt threats to truth. But the most dangerous ones are those that look and sound almost like what you hold dearest.

"Beloved, do not believe every spirit, but test the spirits to see whether they are from God, for many false prophets have gone out into the world" (1 John 4:1). Human words are never the Word. Everything needs to be interpreted: your own intuitions and emotions, public opinion, media reports, and even scriptural interpretation. Everything needs to be tested.

"Perhaps you will recall how," Karl Barth reflects,

> when Hitler used to speak about God, he called Him "the Almighty." But it is not "the Almighty" who is God. . . . We could not better describe and define the Devil than by trying to think this idea of a self-based, free, sovereign ability. This intoxicating thought of

> power is chaos, the *tohu wabohu* which God in His creation has left behind Him, which He rejected when He created heaven and earth. . . . The power of God, real power, is opposed to "power in itself." It is also superior to it; and more, it is its opposite. . . . God is the essence of the possible; but "power in itself" is the essence of the impossible.[1]

The Nazis proclaimed an Aryan Christ, a muscular blonde beast stripped of his Jewish heritage. They raised up the national spirit instead of the Spirit of God. They celebrated Martin Luther as a Teutonic hero who liberated his people from Roman tutelage. Hitler posed in front of churches and spoke of a divine calling to redeem the nation and lead it to greatness. After narrowly escaping assassination attempts, he claimed special protection by the providence of God.

You will have to distinguish all the things: God from idols, faith from ideology, violence from true power, the quiet of fear from true peace, noise from threat. The differences are clear for those who keep their eyes on the cross.

Do not let yourself be deceived by those who under the banner of truth tear down reality: The fruits of the Spirit are "love, joy, peace, patience, kindness, generosity, faithfulness, gentleness, and self-control" (Gal. 5:22–23).

Do not let yourself be deceived by lip service to truth, by committees, by statements, by promises. Sometimes they avoid reality, sometimes they try to hide it. Put them to the test.

Hold onto truth. Disregard for truth is worse than lies. The liar cares about truth and tries to hide it. The bullshitter only cares about persuasion.[2] Bullshitting is quick, easy, and effective: It requires no knowledge, only a goal. Where only persuasion counts, discourse quickly deteriorates into power play. Opinion follows particular trigger paths until we live in different worlds.

If nothing is true, nothing can be done.

Do research. Find facts. Read widely.

Read long rather than short forms. Check several independent sources, right and left, local and national and international.

Seek out contrasting viewpoints and compare differing opinions. Contrast helps to see things more clearly. Barth talked about holding the newspaper in one hand and the Bible in the other.

Discernment is best done in community—not because community achieves consensus, but because community will force you to contend with contrasting experiences and perspectives.

Seek the wisdom of friends and those who are unlike you.

Seek the wisdom of your elders and those who have come long before.

Seek the wisdom of children, the most annoying truth sayers of all.

Seek the wisdom of those on the margins. To them the beast will show its true face first, and they have long had to live with far fewer illusions. To them the resurrected Christ will appear first, and they have long developed practices of resilience and discernment.

Believe the demons, too—they are often the earliest to recognize the Spirit of God. If they flinch and howl, trust that something real is happening. Their violent response is a sign of anxiety and despair, not of true power, but it points you the way. It reveals their weakness and allows you to leverage it.

5

"Wait for the Lord," *or* Confess and Recommit

"God is in control," some will say. "Be silent, be still, wait for the Lord." Sentences like these can excuse inaction, dress paralysis in pious garb, and frame cowardice as an act of faith.

It's true: The psalms urge time and again to "wait for God." But in the psalms, it does not mean "be inactive." It means "do not take revenge." That's a big difference. And when the prophet reminds us, "The LORD is a God of justice; blessed are all those who wait for him" (Isa. 30:18), it is not a command to leave things to God but a reminder to bind ourselves to God's love of justice. "Wait for God" means to watch out for God's action in history and participate in it. Not inaction or surrender, but a renewed commitment.

After the war, the German church confessed its guilt and complicity with the Nazi atrocities in the Stuttgart Declaration of Guilt by stating, "through us has endless suffering been brought to many peoples and countries. What we have often borne witness to before our congregations, we now declare in the name of the whole Church. We have for many years struggled in the name of Jesus Christ against the spirit which found its terrible expression in the National Socialist regime of tyranny, but we accuse ourselves for not witnessing more courageously, for not praying more faithfully, for not believing more joyously, and for not loving more ardently."[1]

This statement was controversial. Many bristled at the idea that they should confess guilt. Had not the church suffered repression and assault on its integrity? Had not thousands of pastors and church officials, and hundreds of thousands of Christians, been killed in the mass murder of Jews, Sinti and Roma, the queer, the disabled, and the politically unaligned? Was the church not victim rather than perpetrator of totalitarian oppression?

To later generations, the statement was controversial for the opposite reason: Was it really a confession of guilt if one only accused oneself of not having done *enough*?

"Wait for the Lord" might today mean to examine our conscience earlier rather than later and to acknowledge with honesty and contrition our shortcomings that have contributed to this moment.

A reckoning is necessary, not to lacerate ourselves while evil triumphs, but to understand and disavow what fuels its rise. Repentance is required, not to add insult to injury, but to reclaim agency by taking responsibility.

On the heels of the tepid Stuttgart Declaration, members of the Confessing Church formulated the further-reaching Darmstadt Statement, admitting: "we went astray when we began to dream about a special German mission as if the German character could heal the sickness of the world. In so doing we prepared the way for the unrestricted exercise of political power, and set our own nation on the throne of God."[2]

They had, the Statement went on, gone astray by wanting to preserve Christian culture against societal changes. They had gone astray in exchanging Christian freedom for conservativism, which enabled the dictatorship. They had gone astray when they forgot about the immanent significance of the gospel and thus failed to center the cause of the poor and marginalized in the coming kingdom of God. Now, they thus called themselves to "in freedom and all soberness realize the responsibility which rests upon us all to rebuild a better form of government in Germany, that shall work for justice and for the welfare, peace, and reconciliation of the nations."[3]

Dietrich Bonhoeffer, reflecting on God's work in and through history, asserts,

> I believe that God can and will let good come out of everything, even the greatest evil. For that to happen, God needs human beings who let everything work out for the best. I believe that in every moment of distress God will give us as much strength to resist as we need. But it is not given to us in advance, lest we rely on ourselves and not on God alone. . . .
>
> I believe that God is no timeless fate but waits for and responds to sincere prayer and responsible actions.[4]

Today, "wait for the Lord" might mean to bind ourselves once more to the God of justice and mercy. It might mean to acknowledge that our strength is not enough, and to offer our sincere prayer. It might mean to take responsibility, examine ourselves, and confess: Where have we, too, dreamed of greatness and exceptionalism? Where have we, too, confused certain cultural formations with our faith commitments, and certain political hopes with the kingdom of God? How have we, too, failed to attend to material injustices and to listen to people who felt increasingly abandoned and precarious?

"Wait for the Lord" means: no excuses. It means confess, recommit—and be reassured: "Wait for the LORD; be strong, and let your heart take courage; wait for the LORD!" (Ps. 27:14).

"God is in control" means: Do not fear. It means take heart—and be confident: "The LORD goes before you. He will be with you; he will not fail you or forsake you. Do not fear or be dismayed" (Deut. 31:8).

6

"Faith, Hope, and Love Remain," *or* Find Purpose

There will be days when you feel that all hope is lost. But hope is not an object that can be misplaced or taken away. Hope is not an emotion that you may or may not feel. Hope is not a positive outlook that may be hard to come by.

Hope is a practice, a discipline, a horizon.

Viktor Frankl observed that even in an environment as terrifying as the concentration camps, people's joy or misery was not directly determined by the surroundings. As people responded differently to their predicament, Frankl observed time and again that those who gave up hope would die very quickly, while those who found ways to cultivate purpose and meaning tended to live on.[1]

Frankl observed three key factors that influenced survival rates: First, projects that let people create things and achieve goals allow for finding purpose through work, accomplishments, and the sense of participating in something greater than themselves.

Second, experience and encounter with other people generate meaning through relationships, love, and shared appreciation of beauty.

Finally, not the degree of suffering but the attitude people adopt toward it leads them to despair or to endure even the greatest hardships.

Oddly, happiness does not always make people happy. Nor does suffering necessarily make people miserable. In fact, wanting to be happy may make people miserable, and finding meaning in suffering can be truly fulfilling.

The Bible does not talk about happiness, but it does talk about joy.

The Bible doesn't offer recipes for avoiding pain and suffering. It lifts up faith, hope, and love.

Which relationships give your actions meaning?

What would you keep doing even if there was no hope for success or improvement?

What commitments are worth embodying even when no one else embodies them?

Your answers to these questions will change how you experience what you experience, what you can or cannot endure. While you cannot choose your situation, you can shape your response. While you may not control the fate of the nation, the community, or even your own feelings, you can lean into faith, hope, and love to find purpose, foster relationships, and generate meaning.

Find your purpose. You don't have to end world hunger or achieve global peace; a purpose only has to be slightly bigger than yourself.

Purpose sends you back to that sense of awe in front of something greater than yourself. It gives you focus. Purpose grounds, inspires, and energizes. It lets you appreciate your own effort and the effort of others. Purpose connects you with those around you: It will lead you to other people, movements and institutions, histories and futures that you can participate in.

"Faith, hope, and love remain," writes Paul, "and the greatest of these is love" (1 Cor. 13:13). Not all is lost when hope is lost. And even hope regenerates when we allow faith and love to sow purpose and meaning.

7

"Two Are Better Than One," *or* Build with What Is There

When you are longing for something new, it is tempting to start from scratch. But doing so will slow you down, isolate you, and dissipate energies.

It takes much longer to build than to destroy, and much destruction is being wrought these days. How can you build on what is already there? What systems are already in place, what resources are already circulating, what pathways and networks have already been forged? How can you stand on them to have stable footing, draw on them to move faster, and build on them to reach higher?

Scavengers are among the most resilient and resourceful species.

Don't reinvent the wheel. Strengthen institutions that already exist. Join spaces that are already constituted. Find legal pathways and follow them as far as they take you. Team up with groups that are already running. Where you can, collaborate. Where you can't, complement. Different approaches can form a division of labor. Different ideas can strengthen one another. Different energies can build momentum.

Activism is not about individual heroism—it is about collective strength.

Power must be built—invest in building up.

Time and ideas are precious—make them last.

Draw on existing resources—and share them with others.

The Christian tradition offers a wealth of such resources: institutions and networks, inherited wisdom and avenues of thought. Use them.

In 1933, the Nazis attempted to integrate all churches in Germany into a centralized structure with a joint constitution under a bishop personally appointed by Hitler. Many pastors and congregations in Germany protested. In June 1934, they came together in Barmen-Gemarke and passed what became known as the Barmen Declaration, a theological statement against the co-optation of the church by the totalitarian state. This assembly included people of different convictions, denominations, and political affiliations, but they worked out of the ecclesial bodies that already existed and gave their own gathering force by understanding themselves as a synod, a church council.

This group came to be known as the Confessing Church because it stood on the confessions of the church to authorize their own prophetic witness. The document they drafted drew on the creeds of the ancient church—scriptural basis, confession of faith, and condemnation of heresies. Even the wording they used echoed the confessions of faith that had wide circulation in their churches.

"Jesus Christ, as he is attested for us in Holy Scripture, is the one Word of God which we have to hear and which we have to trust and obey in life and in death."[1] This first thesis of the Barmen Declaration echoed the widely known first exchange of the Heidelberg Catechism, a document from a sixteenth-century church in the Palatine region of Germany that had since become one of the most circulated confessions of the Reformed churches worldwide: "What is your only comfort in life and in death? That I am not my own, but belong—body and soul, in life and in death—to my faithful Savior, Jesus Christ."[2]

It was this grounding, apparently wholly unpolitical, formulated in a different time and place and for entirely different circumstances, that now allowed them to refuse "other events and powers, figures and truths, as God's revelation." If the church's obedience was to Christ, they insisted, then it could not be ruled by "special leaders [*Führer*] vested with ruling powers."[3]

The Confessing Church spoke in the language of a faith that had been worked out and formulated in other times and places to critique the present; they used documents that had been written in different contexts to transform their own. These traditions allowed the Confessing Church to call existing bodies to attention, helped them discern where to draw the line, lent them words to address their present, and imbued their own declarations with authority.

"Two are better than one because they have a good reward for their toil," knows the Teacher. "For if they fall, one will lift up the other" (Eccles. 4:9–10). The Teacher knows the value of joining forces especially when her mind clouds and darkens. Inventing the wheel for yourself leaves you isolated and weary. Toiling together gives strength and persistence, purpose and force.

Even as you feel lonely and distressed, there will be friends to be found in times such as these. But there are also friends to be found in other times and other places.

Befriend those who would teach you how to live through these times.

Listen to their wisdom.

Let their words and experiences give sharper contours to your own.

Learn from their successes and their failures.

Let them caution and encourage you.

Then put yourself to work so that you would do the same for others.

PART 2

"HEAR THE WORD," OR LISTENING AND RESPONDING

8

"In the Beginning Was the Word," *or* Mind the Power of Language

"In the beginning was the Word . . ." The Bible tells of a word that is literally world-making (John 1:1). But even our small human words make and destroy worlds. Words form perception and engender emotions. Words open up and foreclose opportunities to think, do, and be.

"Sticks and stones may break my bones, but words will never hurt me." The song is an act of defiance: Children know well how much words can hurt, and that bullying rarely stops at name-calling.

Pay attention to language. This is where it starts.

Pay attention when words get switched out or start to change their meaning.

Pay attention when the same stories are told over and over again, and when everyone starts using the same words.

You can see whole wars on the horizon by the way they first show up in language.

Words turn ideas into realities. We have most of our

knowledge from hearsay. Saying something that is false out loud gives it an air of facticity. The more often we hear something said, the more likely we are to believe it.

Words can obfuscate and hide under vague senses of unity. Speaking of "us" and "them" draws attention away from what we have in common or not; all that matters is being part of the "us." Who precisely gets to be "first" by putting "America first"? Against which people are the "enemies of the people" conspiring? If everything is "beautiful," "great," and "huge," what is normal?

Words reveal intentions and stoke action. Chanting "fight, fight, fight" or "never surrender" makes one feel strong and ready to strike. Talking about immigrants as an "invasion" justifies using force rather than due process. Saying that the streets are full of "murderers, rapists, and thugs" legitimates police brutality. Declaring different forms of life "ideology" or "madness" calls for intervention. Portraying threats as "poisoning the blood of our country" necessitates "excising" or even "eliminating" deadly threats.

Violent language prepares the way for violent action.

Pay special attention to dehumanizing language. Talking about people as animals ("dogs," "vermin," "rats") or inanimate things ("tools," "swamp," "waves") changes our attitude toward them. Using nonhuman images erodes connection and empathy. It fosters feelings of contempt and disgust. Such language is a precursor to violence. Of the ten stages of genocide extrapolated from historical evidence, "dehumanization" through language marks stage four.[1]

Words reveal what is inside a person's mind, how they see the world, and how they will interact with it. Words that insult, demean, and ridicule others tell you more about the speaker than about those attacked.

When someone tells you who they are, believe them.

You, too, take care that the way you talk about others and the world reflects who you want to be and how you want to relate. Make sure how you speak makes space for the world you would like to inhabit.

Be wary of slogans.

Ask questions.

Define terms.

Rephrase instead of repeating. Respond instead of reacting.

"The theologian of glory calls evil good and good evil. The theologian of the cross calls the thing what it actually is,"[2] says Martin Luther against those whose language becomes captivated by power.

Speaking the truth means to pronounce things as they really are—the good, the bad, and the ugly. But that requires discernment, too. There is a kind of speech that only outwardly resembles truthfulness. But instead of taking responsibility for reality out of love and care, it destroys reality out of hatred and envy. Instead of proclaiming God's good news and God's judgment, it contradicts the life-giving word of God.

"Speaking the truth must be learned," writes Bonhoeffer.[3] Speaking the truth requires commitment, which has to be achieved and sustained. It requires insight, which has to be discerned and acquired. It requires relationships, which have to be honored and maintained. It requires the right words at the right time, which have to be found and tested.

Practice finding your own words to describe what you see and hear. It will make your thoughts more salient and your perception more acute. Make it a habit. Journal, or record and chronicle in other ways—it lets you see how things are changing, make sense of things, and retain your footing.

Speaking truth to power starts by asking back, "Do you really mean . . . ?"

Mind the power of the word—authoritarian regimes always have. That is why they invent coded language, make up new words, or hide atrocious things under technical or innocuous phrases.

Literary scholar Victor Klemperer documented in his diaries how the language of the Third Reich slowly changed and created the conditions for its gruesome reality.[4] George Orwell drew on Klemperer's insights as he described the "newspeak" of a fictitious dictatorship where "war is peace, freedom is slavery, ignorance is bliss."[5] Ray Bradbury's *Fahrenheit 451* describes a dystopian American future where all books are outlawed.[6]

As books are once more banned, terms fall into disrepute, and whole areas of study are considered dangerous—make sure you know what they contain. If people widely read these books, used these words, studied these topics, the regimes banning them would not last. So study them.

Books are surprisingly hard to control by decree; they can be hid, kept, and circulated without showing up in digital footprints. News articles and social media posts can disappear at the wave of an executive order or the flick of a tech oligarch's wrist. Books give you access to other people's insights and experiences. Books offer bigger and more complex worlds when the language around you diminishes and the world gets smaller.

Read widely and dig deep to find language that you will need: rich and surprising and sprawling and not reducible to the current panic. Your tradition—holy and mundane, literary and cultural, scriptures and confessions—will allow you to think with a richer past and speak to a more promising future.

If you can think and speak beyond the current moment, you can participate in the life that already exists beyond it.

9

"Stand Where God Stands," *or* Protect the Weak

In his prison camp, Dietrich Bonhoeffer writes,

> People turn to God when they are sore bestead;
> pray for help, ask for peace and for bread;
> seek release from being ill, guilty, and dead:
> so do they all, all, Christians and heathens.
>
> People turn to God when He is sore bestead,
> find him poor, scorned, without roof and bread,
> devoured by weakness and sin, near dead:
> Christians stand by God in God's grief.
>
> God turns to all people when they are sore bestead,
> feeds their souls and bodies with God's bread;
> for Christians and heathens at the cross
> God meets death: and gives both of them relief.[1]

What difference does belief in God make in such a time as this? Belief in God is not a comfort in affliction; if anything, it makes injustice and suffering more acute. Belief in God is not a special talisman that will keep you safe, or a miracle weapon that will save the day.

Belief in God is a commitment to stand where God stands.

Because this is where we have found God, this is where God will find us: with our eyes to the cross, staying with the suffering, regardless of our own strengths and weaknesses, hopes and fears.

"God, in a world full of injustice and enmity, is in a special way the God of the destitute, the poor and the wronged," states the Belhar Confession, drawing on Bonhoeffer and the experience of the Confessing Church for its struggle against South African apartheid. Therefore, it concludes, "the church as possession of God must stand where the Lord stands, namely against injustice and with the wronged."[2] Much earlier, Matthew turned this insight into an entire eschatological vision:

> "When the Son of Man comes in his glory . . . [he] will say to those at his right hand, '. . . I was hungry and you gave me food, I was thirsty and you gave me something to drink, I was a stranger and you welcomed me, I was naked and you gave me clothing, I was sick and you took care of me, I was in prison and you visited me.' Then the righteous will answer him, 'Lord, when was it that we saw you hungry and gave you food or

> thirsty and gave you something to drink? And when was it that we saw you a stranger and welcomed you or naked and gave you clothing? And when was it that we saw you sick or in prison and visited you?' And the king will answer them, 'Truly I tell you, just as you did it to one of the least of these brothers and sisters of mine, you did it to me.' . . . Then he will say to those on his left, '. . . truly I tell you, just as you did not do it to one of the least of these, you did not do it to me.'" (25:31–45)

Protect the weak. For Christians, this is not about self-preservation in the long run. It is about following Jesus, who went to the outcasts, and died as one. It is a commitment to remain with those who suffer and to embrace the suffering that might come with it.

Dietrich Bonhoeffer talked about Christ's—and the church's!—"vicarious representative action."[3] Maximilian Kolbe practiced it. When a prisoner escaped from Auschwitz in July 1941, the deputy camp commander, Karl Fritzsch, deterred further escape attempts by randomly picking ten men to be starved to death. One of them cried out, "My wife! My children!" Polish priest and fellow prisoner Maximilian Kolbe volunteered to take his place. He died on August 14, 1941. Franciszek Gajowniczek, whose place he took, survived and lived to the age of ninety-three.

Protect the weak. The good shepherd goes after the one sheep instead of the many. The lost sheep is not the person who hasn't had their come-to-Jesus moment. The lost sheep is the one who, unprotected by the group, will be torn up by the wolves. Don't abandon the few for the supposed good of the many.

We all need God. And God is there for all of us. But those who recognize this are charged with a special responsibility.

We call ourselves Christians not because God belongs to us but because we belong to God.

We call ourselves Christians because we follow Christ the Crucified.

10

"Stand Firm," *or* Don't Give Up Space

"Finally, be strong in the Lord and . . . stand firm," Paul writes to the Ephesians. This is not just a metaphor. Paul is very familiar with struggles in which material and spiritual realities, physical and ideological power, are intertwined. Struggles "against rulers, authorities, and cosmic powers" that are not only "against flesh and blood" but against "spiritual forces in high places" (6:10–13).

Ideology must be resisted by your body in space and time. That is the meaning of corporeal politics.

Don't give up space.

Any space you give up will be used in ways you can no longer influence. Any space you give up might disappear altogether. Your world will become smaller; their world will become bigger. Don't allow that to happen.

In this battle, withdrawing into spaces that are safely like-minded is not gathering strength; it is retreat. So, stand fast. As much as you can, remain "out there" in spaces that are under pressure. Don't pull out of public view. Don't leave your job if it is integrated into an ideological apparatus. Don't give up relationships with people whose opinions you don't share.

Doing so will be uncomfortable. You will feel unproductive, unable to effect change. But your discomfort is not yours alone: It generates friction. You might not change people's minds, but you might be a spark for those who already harbor doubts and second thoughts. Your physical presence will be an obstacle to complete assimilation and unthinking like-mindedness. Sometimes that makes all the difference.

At the 2025 presidential inauguration's prayer service, Episcopal bishop Mariann Edgar Budde closed with "one final plea": "Have mercy, Mr. President, . . . upon the people in our country who are scared now. There are transgender children . . . who fear for their lives [. . . and immigrant children who] fear that their parents will be taken away. . . . May God grant us all the strength and courage to honor the dignity of every human being."[1]

Far from being moved by this appeal to basic humanity, an enraged Trump demanded an apology from the bishop while doubling down on executive orders targeting LGBTQ+ and immigrant communities. A Republican representative even went so far as to call for the bishop to be "added to the deportation list."[2]

Bishop Budde's sermon was not particularly radical or prophetic. She did not openly challenge or defy power; she did not invoke God's judgment or call people to repentance. Every Sunday, there are thousands of sermons from Episcopal pulpits that are more radical in content and tone. Neither was Bishop Budde's sermon particularly successful: It did not persuade the administration to change their policy, and it did not avert their wrath.

What was special about the sermon was that Budde ceded neither physical nor spiritual space to the power that now controlled the room. She practiced corporeal politics. By insisting on staying there and standing firm, she kept space for humanity.

Whatever discomfort she may have experienced, she made Trump and Vance squirm visibly in their seats in front of the cameras. Her act may not have swayed anyone, but it created friction and discomfort for those who wanted to display strength and control, and it encouraged and emboldened thousands of others to similarly stand firm. As her call for humanity echoed without response, it also revealed the inhumanity of their agenda for anyone who would pay attention.

Not giving up space means keeping special watch at the margins. Oppressive politics target the most vulnerable before they turn to the population as a whole. In retrospective, Martin Niemöller, a pastor in the Confessing Church, wrote:

> First they came for the Communists,
> And I did not speak out
> Because I was not a Communist

Then they came for the Socialists
And I did not speak out
Because I was not a Socialist

Then they came for the trade unionists
And I did not speak out
Because I was not a trade unionist

Then they came for the Jews
And I did not speak out
Because I was not a Jew

Then they came for me
And there was no one left
To speak out for me.[3]

With this insight born of hindsight, Niemöller would later participate in writing the Stuttgart Confession of Guilt, in which the church chided itself for not having done enough.

Watch the margins, catch the early signs, and do better.

Stand firm and resist further encroachment.

Protect the weak and shield those who are most vulnerable.

Corporeal politics matter. Creating friction matters. Carrying the burden of visibility for others matters. This is true for public offices and contested spaces. It is true for positions of influence and allies in high places. It is true for your space as well.

However small the space you hold—whether it is a classroom or a barbershop or even just the back of your car—you choose for whom and what the space makes space.

You choose how to inhabit it, how to decorate it, what to display in it.

You choose how to communicate in it.

You choose to go along and not to go along.

If you surrender the space, that decision is already made.

11

"For Such a Time as This," *or* Use Your Privilege

Power corrupts. But power also grants access. Privilege insulates and detaches. But it also enables effective action.

Use whatever power and privilege you have.

The book of Esther tells the story of a young Jewish woman in the Persian diaspora who ends up becoming the wife of King Ahasuerus. Esther learns of a plot by high-ranking officials to murder all Jews in the empire. To reveal the plot to the king, she would have to break his law, punishable by death.

Privilege gives you options.

One option may be to do nothing, to protect yourself. This is understandable. It is also cowardly. Ultimately, it is an illusion. As Esther is torn between protecting her life or that of her people, her cousin reminds her, "Do not think that in the king's palace you will escape any more than all the other Jews" (4:13).

Another option privilege gives is to give up privilege, to have no part in corruption and guilt. Appalled by the hostility against her people, Esther might have decided to leave the king and his court.

It takes moral clarity to recognize one's complicity; it takes courage to renounce one's privilege. But wanting to have no part in what is happening cedes space, access, and power.

As Esther is weighing her options, her cousin asks, "Who knows? Perhaps you have come to royal dignity for just such a time as this" (4:14). Esther takes heart and alerts the king despite the personal risk.

While much of the health system in Nazi Germany endorsed the euthanasia program that sterilized and later murdered people with disabilities and chronic illnesses, some doctors and nurses protected their patients. Clemens von Galen, bishop of Münster and cardinal of the Catholic Church, leveraged the provisions of the Concordat, a treaty that guaranteed the church's rights in Nazi Germany. In widely distributed sermons, he denounced the euthanasia practices so vocally that they were not able to continue in public.

While most of the military supported the war, some of the most notable and effective resistance came from officers' sense of patriotism and duty. General Wilhelm Canaris, a staunch anticommunist, war hero, and onetime enthusiastic National Socialist, became appalled by the war crimes he witnessed in Poland and started conspiring with other high-ranking officers. Under Canaris, the military intelligence service *Abwehr* became a hub of counterintelligence. They gave dissidents cover, helped emigrants, passed military intelligence to foreign powers, and sabotaged the German war effort.

While most of the judiciary was Nazified, some members exploited positions and loopholes to protect people from persecution. Bonhoeffer's brother-in-law, Hans von Dohnanyi, moved in the highest circles of the ministry of justice. He used his access to document their crimes. When he was later assigned to the *Abwehr*, Dohnanyi became part of Canaris's circle. He also protected Bonhoeffer from conscription, arguing that his ecumenical contacts would be useful for the *Abwehr*, where Bonhoeffer soon became a double agent.

Esther's story has a good ending: She saved her people, her own life was spared, and the plotters were put to justice. The Jewish Purim holiday commemorates her brave deed every year. Bishop Galen was protected from retribution by his position and international attention. The Canaris Circle was less lucky. The Nazis executed Dohnanyi, Bonhoeffer, and Canaris only weeks before their reign ended.

Sometimes preserving one's integrity is among the options available to those with sufficient privilege. Esther was able to preserve both her life and her integrity. In her story, the king was good.

But when the head is rotten, personal integrity is also endangered. In his posthumously published *Ethics*, Bonhoeffer even denounces the desire to preserve one's moral purity as a temptation. The only way to stay innocent, he muses, would be to have no part of history. But this would mean having no part of Jesus, who, entering history, took the guilt of all humans upon himself. Jesus's "vicarious representative action," stepping into the place of human sin and taking it upon himself, is demanded of Christians, too. Within history, Bonhoeffer realized, "everyone who acts responsibly, becomes guilty."[1]

Totalitarianism seeks to incorporate all areas of life. That means it will place demands upon you wherever you are—at a court or in a patrol car, in school or at a supermarket counter, in a state park or in a research institution. No conscientious objection or dropping out of human society can spare you from responsibility and guilt.

The question is not: How do you stay morally pure? The question is: What is the best possible use of the power entrusted to you?

Totalitarianism seeks to incorporate all areas of life. That also means all areas of life become sites of resistance. For children to keep learning something other than propaganda, teachers must remain at public schools. For people facing legal charges for political reasons, lawyers need to keep advocating. For health services to stay available to trans, chronically ill, and disabled people, doctors must write scripts. Courts must continue to review executive orders. Diplomats must keep liaising with other countries. Military officers, prison guards, postal workers, nurses, counselors, cashiers, cleaners, operation managers, data scientists, engineers—all will have to draw lines and make creative use of the space and agency they have.

Resigning when your institution is corrupt may preserve your integrity and dignity. But nothing more. It will be more important than ever that people remain who will not simply follow orders. In times of mortal danger, what you can do is more important than keeping your hands clean.

Don't bury your talents in the hope of saving yourself. Spend them.

Don't throw them away to keep your hands clean. Invest them.

Don't give up your privilege, don't hide behind it. Put it to work.

You will resist most effectively where you have the most experience and knowledge, the best networks and connections, the furthest access and reach. Maybe, like Esther, God has given them to you "for such a time as this."

12

"Obey God More Than Humans," *or* Draw Lines

"Most of the power of authoritarianism is freely given," finds Timothy Snyder, who studied authoritarian systems of the twentieth century his entire career. "Individuals think ahead about what the more repressive government will want, and then offer themselves without being asked. A citizen who adapts in this way is teaching power what it can do."[1]

The phenomenon Snyder describes is called "anticipatory obedience": People are extremely perceptive to changes in power and adapt nimbly. Fearing exposure or retaliation, anticipating opportunities and rewards, or simply picking up cues and vibes, they anticipate the desires of those in power and behave accordingly.

An itinerant Abraham might have felt his lack of protection against power acutely. When traveling through the territory of powerful men whom he suspected of desiring his beautiful wife, he passed her off as his sister. By trying to keep himself safe, he effectively told them that they could take her with impunity—and they did. Twice the story repeats itself, even as twice it turns out that Abraham's unsolicited surrender and "sacrifice" (of Sarah!) was neither expected nor demanded (Gen. 12; Gen. 20).

Whether chosen to "get on the good side" of those in power in the hope of getting a piece of their pie, or out of fear of retaliation, anticipatory obedience allows authoritarian powers to reign with surprisingly little force. People behave as if these leaders had unlimited power, which effectively gives them that power without having to work (read: exercise force) for it. Don't make things that easy for them.

Don't obey in advance.

Don't obey more than you have to.

Don't teach power what it can do.

Draw conscious limits around the commands you will or will not obey.

Luke reports:

> So they watched [Jesus] and sent spies who pretended to be honest, in order to trap him by what he said and then to hand him over to the jurisdiction and authority of the governor. So they asked him, "Teacher, . . . is it lawful for us to pay tribute to Caesar or not?" But he perceived their craftiness and said to them, "Show me a denarius. Whose head and whose title does it bear?" They said, "Caesar's." He said to them, "Then give to Caesar the things that are Caesar's and to God the things that are God's." And they were not able in

> the presence of the people to trap him by what he said, and being amazed by his answer they became silent. (20:20–26)

Jesus's cautious "Give to Caesar the things that are Caesar's" is complemented by his firm "and to God the things that are God's." This posture is different from anticipatory obedience. It draws a line—what authorities may or may not rightly demand—and commits to not crossing that line.

The Roman Empire well understood that this posture undermined their claim to power as much as a call to arms would have—this is why they chose crucifixion as the method of execution for Jesus, the capital punishment for insurrectionists. But his response did not give them the pretext for arrest that a call to arms would have. It eventually took the outrage of religious leaders and the betrayal by one of his closest friends to seal Jesus's fate.

What in Luke's Gospel remains an implicit stance, Acts expresses in positive terms. As the apostles are brought before the council of Jerusalem, they profess: "We must obey God rather than any human authority" (5:29). Similarly, the Barmen Declaration announces: "Jesus Christ, as he is attested for us in Holy Scripture, is the one Word of God which we have to hear and which we have to trust and obey in life and in death," subsequently denouncing any ultimate claims by "other events and powers, figures and truths." Against the total claim of the totalitarian state, Barmen refused to let God's claim on us be compartmentalized and limited, “as though there were areas of our life in which we would not belong to Jesus Christ, but to other lords.”[2]

Gain clarity ahead of time where your allegiances lie.

What commitments must you keep?

What lines will you not cross?

13

"Be Wise as Serpents and Innocent as Doves," *or* Choose Your Battles and Avoid Traps

In Luke's story, those who ask Jesus about taxes are trying to set a trap. The world will be full of these traps. Authoritarian leaders demand full obedience, and totalitarian regimes will actively seek to eliminate friction in all areas of life.

Jesus did not attempt to escape arrest and crucifixion. He kept teaching and living a different kingdom than the reigning political theologies until he was charged with blasphemy and sedition. But he did avoid being arrested on bullshit charges. And as he charged his disciples with proclaiming his word, he also cautioned them, "I am sending you out like sheep into the midst of wolves, so be wise as serpents and innocent as doves" (Matt. 10:16).

Be brave, but avoid traps.

Speak truth boldly, but choose your battles wisely.

The three wise men avoided the choice of either becoming martyrs or delivering an innocent babe to a bloodthirsty emperor; they simply traveled a different route than the one that led through Jerusalem. Jesus was crucified for blasphemy and sedition because of his teaching and ministry. But he didn't make it easy for his opponents by refusing to pay taxes.

Be wary of displays and confrontations that make little effective difference.

Avoid unnecessary risks.

Be mindful what might be used against you.

Maurice Bavaud, a Swiss theology student who attempted to assassinate Hitler in 1938, was arrested for traveling without proper documents. Hans von Dohnanyi, who was involved in several attempted assassinations and coups d'état, was arrested for foreign currency violations. Once imprisoned, both were executed by the Nazis. Don't make it so easy for them.

Decide which roads you might not need to travel.

Avoid speeding tickets, broken taillights, and lapsed registrations.

Have your documents and legal issues in order.

Pay your taxes and your child support.

Understand which symbolic stances, key words, and affiliations are being weaponized, and how social media posts, drug and porn use, and extramarital affairs can be used against you.

Make no mistake: Trying to achieve invulnerability would be the worst form of "anticipatory obedience" to totalitarian grasp. It is impossible to lead your life in such a way that nothing can be used against you by those with ill will and sufficient resources.

But when making decisions, ask yourself: Will this make it harder for them to do bad things, or will it just make it easier for them to target me?

Be strategic in your choice of measures and media. Where possible, prefer legal over illegal, and nonviolent over violent forms of resistance. Minimizing risk will contribute to sustainability and long-term effectiveness.

Put in unencrypted emails only what you would feel comfortable having cited in the local newspaper or in court.

Post on social media only what you would also be happy to write on a flag in front of your house. Posts can not only be spotted by ill-meaning passersby but automatically crawled by bots.

That doesn't mean you should stop communicating. But communicate to organize, not to signal. And choose degrees of publicness and risk as you do. Consider stating your opinions in a medium that gives you more control over circulation and interpretation.

Jesus taught in person.

14

"Do Something Brave," *or* Make a Start

"It is not enough to be against it, you have to do something against it," wrote Sophie Scholl. Scholl's sentiment echoes that of Swiss reformer Huldrych Zwingli four centuries earlier. When Catholic forces attacked Reformed Zürich in 1531, Zwingli enlisted as a soldier and allegedly admonished those around him, "For God's sake, do something brave."[1]

Whether Zwingli's belligerent bravery was the truest witness or wisest choice might be debated. Scholl practiced a less violent courage. As a twenty-one-year-old, she joined the White Rose, a student group that wrote and distributed leaflets against the regime. They openly denounced the Nazi oppression, mass murder of the Jews, and doomed war effort. Appealing to their fellow citizens' conscience and sense of shame, they called for resistance.

Together with her brother Hans, Sophie Scholl was caught dropping antiwar fliers at the University of Munich in 1943. In front of a hastily convened trial that was later declared a judicial murder, Sophie explained herself:

"Somebody, after all, had to make a start. What we wrote and said—many others believe the same things. They just don't dare express themselves as we did."[2]

Somebody has to make a start. It is hard to stand out. It is certainly risky. Sophie Scholl was executed on the day of the trial, almost as if the Nazis feared her courage could become contagious.

Somebody has to make a start. The more people remain silent, the harder it is to speak out—especially in an environment that cultivates conformity and compliance through terror and propaganda. Gestapo reports suggest that less than 5 percent of the German population actively opposed the Nazis through acts of resistance or conspiracy. But historians also estimate that ideologically committed and actively practicing Nazis amounted to only about 5–10 percent of the population, with another 20–30 percent generally approving of their policies. Scholl lucidly saw: "The real damage is done by those millions who want to 'survive.' The honest men who just want to be left in peace. Those who don't want their little lives disturbed by anything bigger than themselves. . . . Those who don't like to make waves—or enemies. . . . If you don't make any noise, the bogeyman won't find you. But it's all an illusion because they die too, those people who roll up their spirits into tiny little balls so as to be safe. Safe?! From what? Life is always on the edge of death."[3] The Nazis never were in the majority. Those who simply "went along" were absolutely critical to the regime's success.

Scholars quibble over exact numbers: how many held or internalized antisemitic sentiments; how many were genuinely indifferent, opportunistic, or scared; how many were silently uncomfortable with Nazi politics; how hard it was for the committed Nazis to keep the general population compliant. But the "bandwagon effect" is well documented: In self-reinforcing trends, people take up beliefs, ideas, and practices they witness around them.[4] And it doesn't only work for Nazis, either.

It is easier for you to speak up and stand out if you see others already doing so. So, find these others. Run with them.

Let their example strengthen your resolve.

Then, be such an Other for others, in turn.

God reassures Paul through a vision: "Do not be afraid, but speak and do not be silent, for I am with you, and no one will lay a hand on you to harm you, for there are many in this city who are my people" (Acts 18:9–10).

The longer you remain silent, the more difficult it becomes to speak. Now, you are not only up against the evils you denounce, but also against your earlier self. If you didn't speak then, why speak now?

But your silence will not protect you. Not from harm, not from moral complicity.

Not speaking out does not make you neutral. It makes you a *bystander*. The main moral difference is not between perpetrators and victims but between those who choose action and those who look on. Bystanders enable cycles of violence and systemic injustice to go unchecked. No system of oppression can succeed at scale without bystanders.

Indifference is consent to what is happening. Inaction is a choice to leave it unchallenged. Under conditions of injustice and violence, there is no neutrality, only active resistance or enablement.

"The sad truth is that most evil is done by people who never make up their minds to be good or evil," philosopher Hannah Arendt diagnosed at the trial of Adolf Eichmann, the SS officer who had logistically managed and overseen the mass deportation of Jews to extermination camps across Europe.[5] This man was personally responsible for the murder of millions. Yet what distinguished him, Arendt found, was no special hatred but simply the avoidance of critical thinking and moral contemplation.

Eichmann followed orders out of a sense of duty and took pride in formally fulfilling them. The "banality of evil," Arendt saw, was that even the greatest atrocities do not need fanatics or monsters. It suffices that ordinary people neglect to reflect and fail to resist actively.

More important than being a hero is choosing to not go along. It might not require exceptional bravery to take up arms if everyone else is also fighting. Even great costs can be bearable if rewarded by approval or public admiration. It requires more bravery to refuse to march when ordered to do so.

Much smaller risks can be much harder to take when they make you stand out. Under certain circumstances, it takes exceptional courage to remain seated, to pass on a note, to hold up a sign or wear a lapel pin, or even to ask a question.

Think for yourself.

Make your own choices.

Be as brave as you can, as early as you can.

Expect to be uncomfortable.

Question duty, procedure, and formality. Make it a habit to ask "why?," "what are the other options?," and once more "why?"

Practice what you anticipate before it happens, in your head or with trusted friends. Do so often, and you will snap out of inactivity faster.

If you find yourself unsure how to act, at least say loudly, "This seems wrong," or "That sounds racist," or "Are you okay?" or "I don't understand why we should do this." Take notes. Record. Share information.

If you are scared to intervene or confront, distract and diffuse instead. Shout "Fire!," break into song or conversation, play the bumbling fool. It can be more effective to look ridiculous or clueless than to die a hero.

But for God's sake, don't be a bystander.

PART 3

“BECOME WHAT YOU HAVE RECEIVED,” OR COMMUNION

15

"Rejoice Always," *or* Lean into Joy

There is a second contender for shortest verse in the Bible. In the English translation, it is "Jesus wept" (John 11:35 KJV).[1] In the original Greek, it is "Rejoice always" (1 Thess. 5:16).

It is important, the Teacher knows, to make space and time for both "a time to weep and a time to laugh" (Eccles. 3:4). Paul, too, exhorts believers to "Rejoice with those who rejoice; weep with those who weep" (Rom. 12:15).

From delighting in creation to celebrating liberation, transformation, and new creation, joy is the first, the last, and the greatest response to God's work. The Westminster Catechism even postulates as the purpose of human existence "to glorify God and to enjoy Him forever."[2]

Like her namesake Esther, the biblical queen who saved her people from genocide, Esther "Etty" Hillesum refused to choose her own safety over that of her fellow Jews. When the Nazis started rounding up Jews in Amsterdam, the young Dutch woman voluntarily took on administrative duties at Westerbork transit camp, to support those facing deportation and document their experiences. Soon the Nazis revoked her personnel status. Etty was herself interned, put on a train, and murdered in Auschwitz on November 30, 1943.

Etty's posthumously published diaries brim with joy, hope, and delight. From occupied Amsterdam, she writes, "Life is beautiful. And I believe in God. And I want to be right in the thick of what people call 'horror' and still be able to say, 'life is beautiful.'"[3]

Etty marveled at the indestructible beauty of the world at her window, and of her own soul: "Somewhere inside of me the jasmine continues to blossom undisturbed, just as profusely and delicately as it ever did. And it spreads its scent round the house where you dwell, oh God. . . . I bring You not only my tears and my forebodings on this stormy, gray, Sunday morning, I even bring you scented jasmine. And I shall bring you all the flowers I meet along my way, and truly there are many of those."[4]

As she was being transported to her death, Etty threw a postcard from the train that read, "Opening the Bible at random I find this: 'The Lord is my high tower.' I am sitting on my rucksack in the middle of a full freight car. Father, Mother, and Mischa are a few cars away. In the end, the departure came without warning [but] we left the camp singing." She closes, to the unknown finder of the postcard, "Thank you all for your kindness and care."[5]

As she chronicled the mounting horrors around her, Etty refused to confine her emotional energy to anger or despair. She reveled in fierce mystic spirituality, insatiable erotic love, and celebration of beauty. Etty saw lucidly that each one depended on the other: "Life may be brimming over with experiences, but somewhere, deep inside, all of us carry a vast and fruitful loneliness wherever we go. And sometimes the most important thing in a whole day is the rest we take between two deep breaths, or the turning inward in prayer for five short minutes."[6]

For Etty, such turning inward became the most important work to quell hatred and destruction. Our main responsibility, she found, was "to guard little pieces of God inside of [our]self," and our "one moral duty . . . to reclaim large areas of peace in ourselves, more and more peace, and to reflect it toward others. And the more peace there is in us, the more peace there will also be in our troubled world."[7]

Etty's biographer reckons that "it was her practice of paying deep attention which transformed her" from a rather self-centered person to one who radiated empathy, peace, and resilience.[8] Etty Hillesum did not let the horrors of her day define who she was, nor did she let them exhaust the meaning of her life.

Terror inspires fear and rules by fear. One of the most persistent refrains of the Bible is "Do not be afraid." The horror is real, but it is not the only thing that is true.

Joy comes before, endures throughout, and comes after terror.

Joy is the radiance of the grace of every new morning's dawn.

Joy despite and beyond despair is its own testimony that suffering cannot determine what your life is about or what your life is for.

Joy despite and beyond suffering is its own testimony to God's sovereignty over the powers that be.

"The joy of the Lord is your strength," proclaims Nehemiah to the people of God gathered in the square (Neh. 8:10). Returned from exile, having rebuilt Jerusalem, they hear the promise of God anew. The grief and pain still lingering in their bones mix with remembrance and anticipation.

Nehemiah, a eunuch for the sake of this office of governance, commands them, "Go your way, eat the fat and drink sweet wine and send portions of them to those for whom nothing is prepared" (8:10). Leaning into joy is the best protection against building new walls and erecting higher boundaries. Joy protects you from trauma reactions that will harden your heart more than they can ever keep you safe.

Guard little pieces of God.

Guard little pieces of joy.

Look further around you, look deeper inside you, at all that is there that does not bear the name of suffering.

Behold the sparrows, behold the trees, all beings whose glory is much shorter- or longer-lived than what you think of as a historic moment.

Pay attention to your body, your mind, your heart, your friends and chosen family, your miraculous encounters. Where do joy, glory, and gratitude break through gloom and suffering in your own life?

Make space for that joy and let it grow.

Let it roar through your life and expand ever further.

Laugh vibrantly, celebrate unabashedly, enjoy fully, and love without constraint.

16

"Pray Without Ceasing," *or* Fortify Interiority

"Rejoice always," Paul writes in his first preserved letter, and he continues, "pray without ceasing, give thanks in all circumstances, for this is the will of God in Christ Jesus for you. Do not quench the Spirit. Do not despise prophecies, but test everything; hold fast to what is good; abstain from every form of evil" (1 Thess. 5:16–22). These things belong together: Cultivating joy and gratitude requires discernment and boundary drawing.

Protect your joy.

Protect your integrity.

Protect your privacy.

A private life is not the opposite of a public life; it is its condition. A life lived in public quickly gets washed out and worn thin. Privacy offers the safe space that is necessary to reflect and discern, and the shield under which depth and integrity bloom.

Cultivate a rich private life and protect it fiercely—especially if your vocation requires a certain degree of publicness.

The Nazis were among the first regimes who were able to enter people's bedrooms and living rooms through mass media. Technological progress has since turned unilateral broadcasting into social media's multisided flow of information and representation. But your ability to upload rather than just receive content does not necessarily lead to mutuality and empowerment; it also complements propaganda with surveillance.

Keep the personal personal.

Protect sensitive information—your own and that of others.

Practice data minimalism.

Use encrypted messaging services and VPN[1] clients. Shred documents before putting them into the trash. Use discretion in what apps you need and to what data you give them access.

Be intentional in your choice of media and breadth of distribution. Could this email have been a meeting? Should this public post have been a direct message? Or a newsletter?

Even those of us whose work demands publicity must ask ourselves, are you communicating something specific to specific someones—or are you just posting out of inner restlessness? Are you building relationships—or are you just skywriting to not feel disconnected? Are you listening and speaking—or just drowning out silence with chatter?

Jesus did not preach a different message to the public than to his disciples. But he frequently withdrew from the crowd into an inner circle, and he distinguished between how and what he shared in the marketplace and around the dinner table. Jesus also frequently withdrew into solitude to pray.

Prayer is that most intimate of spaces that you share with God alone.

Cultivate a private life before and beyond exposing your intimate thoughts, feelings, and commitments to the world's scrutinizing eyes and ears. Cultivate intimacy, silence, prayer, and solitude.

In *The Origins of Totalitarianism*, Hannah Arendt finds that one of the main enablers for a politics of intolerance was widespread loneliness. Loneliness is different from solitude. Solitude requires hospitality to one's own feelings and thoughts, and a certain level of comfort with them. Solitude grounds and centers. It cultivates friendship with oneself and thus prepares us to connect with others in openness and generosity, too.

Loneliness is the opposite. It wears away the ability to empathize, to engage in rational discourse and critical thought. It leads to despair, misjudgment, and the instrumentalization of other people. Social media is full of loneliness, of an eroded sociality in which people lose connection with others and with reality. Dietrich Bonhoeffer cautions, "Those who want community without solitude plunge into the void of words and feelings, and those who seek solitude without community perish in the bottomless pit of vanity, self-infatuation, and despair. Whoever cannot be alone should beware of community. Whoever cannot stand being in community should beware of being alone."[2]

The capacity to be alone and the capacity to be with one another are not mutually exclusive. They strengthen one another. But too often we escape from one to the other and thus lose both.

Flee loneliness, and flee crowd bathing.

Seek solitude in order to be able to find community—with yourself as well as with others.

Make time and space for prayer, for grounding, for examination, for critical thinking.

Make space for silence. It expands your ability to listen and your ability to speak: the right words, at the right time, to the right person.

17

"Break Bread," *or* Nourish Community

The book of Acts describes the life of early Christians—before there was an institutionalized structure or even a name like "church"—like this: "All who believed were together and had all things in common; they would sell their possessions and goods and distribute the proceeds to all, as any had need. Day by day, as they spent much time together in the temple, they broke bread at home and ate their food with glad and generous hearts, praising God and having the goodwill of all the people" (Acts 2:44–47). These words give testimony of an amazing community. But real community is always a source of amazement. It cannot be taken for granted. Not in one's family of origin, not in one's neighborhood, not in one's polity.

Kinship cannot be decreed by ties of blood or land, passports or creeds. But where we find it, real community encounters us as a miracle and transforms us into new beings.

Real community, Bonhoeffer writes in *Life Together*, is "a gift of grace from the kingdom of God, which can be taken away from us any day." Amid desolation and loneliness, "the physical presence of other Christians is a source of incomparable joy and strength to the believer."[1]

For Bonhoeffer, the church is not a building, but it is also not a people. It is the body of Christ.

We enter into bodily communion with Christ and with one another as we break bread. The bodily unity is Christ's, and only in Christ are we unified. Even so, this communion becomes visible and actual in our embodied life, our physical presence, and our solidarity with one another.

Real community is a miracle, but it is not extraordinary. Christ is crucified. The body into which we are incorporated by breaking bread is a broken body.

Those who desire idealized, unbroken relationships with idealized, unbroken human beings destroy the real body of Christ instead of building it. Judas's "betrayal" of Jesus, scholars suspect, was most likely his attempt to force the revolutionary turn he idealized.

Idealized community invariably produces shadows of exclusion, violence, and despair. In Acts, the miracle of Christian community is immediately endangered by the need to navigate the shortcomings of real people against idealistic standards. Ananias and Sapphira fall down dead as they find themselves unable to live up to an ideal community.

Do not set your heart on a particular vision of community. The greatest danger to real community is the wishful image of ideal community. The sooner we embrace the necessary disillusionment of idealized community, the sooner we can embrace one another.

"Christian community is not an ideal, but a divine reality," Bonhoeffer writes, "not an ideal we have to realize, but rather a reality created by God in Christ in which we may participate. The more clearly we learn to recognize that the ground and strength and promise of all our community is in Jesus Christ alone, the more calmly we will learn to think about our community and pray and hope for it."[2]

Bonhoeffer's small book *Life Together* itself emerges out of an intentional Christian community built on the edge of terror. As the nationalistic German Christians increasingly self-aligned with the Nazi regime and created their own version of an ideal community, the Confessing Church developed into an oppositional community with independent, partially underground structures. Bonhoeffer was charged with running a theological seminary at Finkenwalde. The book emerges from this experience of an intentional, life-giving community, under pressure from outside threats and inside disillusionment, and soon declared illegal by the regime.

The community we experience will always be limited, and it will always be temporary.

Against the straitjacket of the world, intentional community practices utopian imagination, however long it lasts. Practical constraints narrow the horizon. Stretch what is possible by stretching what you rehearse in prayer and imagination. The fifth-century axiom *lex orandi, lex credendi* establishes the following: Not what we believe determines what we do, but how we pray informs what we believe, love, and hope. Without imagination, we are confined to what is.

Intentional community participates in God's reality in the midst of this reality. It enacts and expands the body into which we are engrafted by the flesh and blood of real people with all their wonder and doubt, strength and shortcomings.

We enact and expand this body as we break bread.

We tap into a different world as we share cups of blessing and remembrance.

Sing songs of joy and sorrow.

Tell stories full of wonder and doubt.

Listen to one another.

Gather the living. Mourn the dead.

Attend to the sick and imprisoned. Write letters of support for people far away. Collect money for people we have never met.

Caution and encourage one another.

Pray for one another.

Nothing can be taken for granted; everything depends on these practices.

18

"Do This in Remembrance of Me," *or* Rehearse Dangerous Memories

It makes a difference which histories we remember and how we remember them. The pasts we narrate color our present and shape our future.

Pay attention to which names get attached to buildings and landscapes, and which are taken off.

Pay attention to which murals are painted over and which memorials are erected.

Pay attention to whose stories are erased and whose are celebrated.

Memory is a tricky thing. It can fuel nostalgia, inertia, and reaction. But it can also give your love depth and your vision breadth. It can haunt the present with shame and blame, but also enrich it with gratitude and grief. It can engender feelings of powerlessness or renew agency. It has to be practiced consciously, or else it will gnaw away at your subconscious.

Practice memory intentionally, gently, communally.

Absences constitute and haunt all community, and will assert their presence in its midst. Nowhere is this more blatantly disconcerting, and more confusingly comforting, than in the Last Supper.

"Do this in remembrance of me," a Jesus anticipating his own death exhorts an intimate gathering of friends (1 Cor. 11:24; Luke 22:19). Soon, they will be brought even closer as they mourn his absence by ritually re-creating this scene. Now, the perfect presence is wrinkled by the inclusion of the one who will betray him. Judas sits at the table, puts his hand into the same bowl. Breaking bread with him, Jesus incorporates Judas into the body that the disciple breaks.

"Do this in remembrance of me." Jesus invites you to commemorate his betrayal, death, and resurrection. His invitation makes space for "dangerous memory," a memory that, as post-Holocaust Catholic theologian Johann Baptist Metz tells us, "puts pressure on and questions our present because in it we remember an unfinished future."[1] Memory can unsettle the unreconciled present and open up a future for the hopeless and the forgotten, the failed and the oppressed.

Jesus invites you to perform such recollection of dangerous memory with your whole body, as a community: As you eat and drink and recount the stories, you re-member the body, putting the members of the body back together into a fellowship.

Re-member the body.

Remember horrors to create pathways to survival.

Remember inhumanity to make space for humanity.

Remember to hold accountable, remember to enable a different future.

Re-member: You are sustained and embraced.

Remembering keeps the ghosts alive so that they can warn and comfort, haunt and inspire the living: dangerous memories that push toward an unfinished future. Making the absent present allows for processing grief, strengthening commitments, and opening up vision. Such remembrance commits you to work for a future for those who have been forgotten, erased, and left behind.

Jews have long practiced dangerous memories, retelling the story of the exodus, a story of suffering and hope, of loss and promise. God liberates a people from enslavement, delivers them from the wilderness, and makes a way out of no way: life out of death. After Auschwitz, remembrance became the practice of insisting "never again": "The premier demand upon all education is that Auschwitz not happen again," postulated Theodor Adorno of the Frankfurt School of Critical Theory.[2]

Remember those who are absent. Remember those who have come before you, those who have left, and those who have been taken away. Recall their faces. Name their names. Tell their stories. Eat their foods. Dream their dreams. Weave their absence into your presence; it will thicken your social fabric. Their souls will nourish yours.

Use memory to create empathy, not to immunize yourself.

Use memory to enlarge your capacity to feel, to care, and to dream.

Use memory not to bind yourself to the past, but to make a future possible.

"Never again" means "never again for anyone."[3]

19

"When Your Children Ask You . . . ," *or* Be a Little Conservative

Honor your ancestors; talk to your children. Taking responsibility is about responding to the past and preparing for the future in the present. "When your children ask you in the time to come, 'What is the meaning of the decrees and the statutes and the ordinances that the LORD our God has commanded you?'" be prepared to answer them (Deut. 6:20).

In his imprisonment, Bonhoeffer reflects: "The ultimately responsible question is not how I extricate myself heroically from a situation but [how] a coming generation is to go on living. Only from such a historically responsible question will fruitful solutions arise, however humiliating they may be for the moment. In short, it is much easier to see a situation through on the basis of principle than in concrete responsibility. The younger generation will always have the surest sense whether an action is done merely in terms of principle or from living responsibly, for it is their future that is at stake."[1]

It takes a village to raise a child. For which children are you part of the village? Take responsibility, respond to them.

Swedish postwar author Astrid Lindgren wrote stunning children's books, including the tales of one Pippi Longstocking. Her stories unapologetically engage with death and terror, illness and disability, abandonment and fear, courage and even suicide. They are also utterly unprincipled, full of joy, creativity, and wildness. As these stories help children process hard questions, they also uplift childlike virtues.

Naïveté refuses to conform to what has become normal.

Humor and wit break through the tyranny of fear.

Empathy gets under the skin of a hard-boiled world.

Curiosity and wonder discover alternatives to the inevitable.

In one of Lindgren's books, one child tells another in the face of certain death, "But there are things you have to do, otherwise, you're not a human being, just a piece of dirt."[2] You cannot protect future generations from fear and darkness. But you can respond to them with the seriousness that their questions, desires, and confusions deserve. Don't belittle them. Talk to them, learn from them, and raise them to be strong adults who will equally take responsibility.

Some of the most notable opposition in the Third Reich emerged on conservative grounds. Many of the figures who actively conspired and organized against the regime came from aristocratic families, military leadership, and educated bourgeois elites who found their conscience and steeled their spine.

The circle around Claus von Stauffenberg is a prime example of conservatives who broke their oath of allegiance to the Führer out of their sense of duty to God and nation, military honor, or belief in natural law. Dietrich Bonhoeffer, too, was part of this group; his execution resulted from their conspiration to assassinate Hitler, the famous but failed "20 July plot."

Conservative values can be truly radical when those in power do not care to sustain what makes shared life possible: When people "move fast and break things," decency and kindness insist on the humanity of those otherwise crushed under the wheels. Even decorum and politeness can be radical in a world that scoffs at empathy. Honor and courage are necessary to confront injustice and violence. Liberty is not an excuse for only caring about yourself, but a commitment to liberate others.

"Radicalism" is about roots. "Conservatism" is about preservation. Faithfulness to living truth becomes brittle when either turns into a principle. The question is not whether you call yourself conservative or radical, the question is: On which roots are you drawing strength, and what are you working to preserve? What is the meaning of the stories you tell and the values you have inherited? What will you do to make a future possible in which you are called on to respond?

Be radical, and draw on your roots.

Be conservative, preserve what is needed for a different future.

Be radical and conservative: Lose your principles and take responsibility.

20

"Many Members," *or* Value Different Gifts

"Teacher," reports John to Jesus, "we saw someone casting out demons in your name, and we tried to stop him because he was not following us" (Mark 9:38). If you want to take all the credit, you will burn out doing all the work. If you work only with those who come from where you come from, believe what you believe, and want what you want, you will find yourself alone.

"Do not stop him," Jesus corrects John and notes, "whoever is not against us is for us" (Mark 9:39–40). If you seek good wherever you can find it, you will find that we are many. You will find unexpected collaborators in people of different beliefs and motivations, and form surprising alliances with people of different goals.

Seek solidarity, not purity.

Cherish multiplicity and diversity, even where it is inconvenient.

Diversity of opinion is unruly, but unruliness is a powerful resource in an age where everyone is meant to go along. It produces disruptions, and it produces new insights.

Diversity offers a wealth of gifts. You may respond with suspicion—or envy—to people who think different thoughts, talk different talks, organize different actions, or prioritize different goals. You will miss out on the gifts they offer to the larger body. As Paul teaches: "Now there are varieties of gifts but the same Spirit, and there are varieties of services but the same Lord, and there are varieties of activities, but it is the same God who activates all of them in everyone. To each is given the manifestation of the Spirit for the common good" (1 Cor. 12:4–7).

Discern the Spirit, embrace the gifts, build the body.

Seek solidarity, not purity. Just because you have to protect yourself, not everyone should lay low. Just because you are comfortable with taking extraordinary risks, not everyone can afford to.

Some will hide; some will speak out fearlessly.

Some will put their bodies on the line; some will move out of the way.

Some will renounce their privilege to protect their integrity; some will be able to use their privilege in spaces of power; some will defy and challenge those same powers.

Don't be defensive about what you can or cannot do, and don't judge others for being in a different place than you are. Don't charge the eye with not being an ear. "If all were a single member, where would the body be? As it is, there are many members yet one body. The eye cannot say to the hand, 'I have no need of you,' nor again the head to the feet, 'I have no need of you'" (1 Cor. 12:19–21).

Different members have different kinds of exposure and

different risks to injury. Different members have different insights, functions, ranges, and possibilities of action. That is not a lack of unity but an opportunity for effective divisions of labor.

Seek solidarity, not likeness. For the body to go anywhere, some have to do the walking, some have to do the balancing, some have to do the watching out. We need one another's gifts and contributions.

For some to practice civil disobedience, others have to design fliers and cook meals.

For some to harbor refugees in their basement, others have to take out trash and laundry, offer financial and moral support.

For some to get access to medical care, others have to cross state lines.

For some to go to prison for their beliefs, others have to give legal counsel, run messages, and keep up care work and organizing.

Some parts of the body will have to expose themselves or get dirty; some parts of the body will have to be hidden and protected.

Some may have to die as heroes, but many, many more have to live.

"One body, many members" is a wonderful image for Christian existence and for the church. It also applies to institutions at large. A body is more than the sum of its individual members. Authoritarians know this. That's why they seek to dismantle institutions.

Institutions are imperfect, frustrating, and slow. They

turn insights, movements, and energies into structures and processes. They are inherently conservative. In times of peace and order, institutions tend to not work in favor of the marginalized. But against the destructive tidal waves of authoritarianism, nothing offers protection like the inertia of institutions, their inherited knowledge, their professional ethics, their established networks, their distinction between role and person.

Individuals can hide behind offices.

Integrity can be preserved through following process.

Red tape can be used to stall chaos and destruction.

Even in a conquered Europe, Danish bureaucracy held up the Nazis until the Jewish population had been safely evacuated. When Nazis banned higher education in Poland, Polish universities went underground, keeping their established formats running in secret and preserving intellectual life. Norwegian public schools refused to comply with the imposition of Nazi ideology. When twelve thousand teachers resigned, many of them were arrested, but the public support was so overwhelming that the Nazis backed down.

The body is more than the sum of its individual members. The body can protect individual members as a body, and it can even survive them. Protect the body, so it can protect the members.

21

"One Body," *or* Hold onto Unity

Hold onto unity, but mistrust uniformity. A living body will be composed of many different members and marvelously unruly functions.

The Nazis loved to speak about the *Volkskörper*, the collective body of the people, and pursued a political program of *Gleichschaltung*, the ideological alignment of all members and synchronization of all functions of the collective body. They portrayed various groups as "parasites," "diseases," "impurities," and "corruptions" of this body, and strove to "cleanse" the nation from them.

It is a remarkable fact of history that precisely in the age of world wars, of unprecedented nationalism and military aggression, of ideologies of purity and conformity, an ecumenical movement thrived. It was neither a remedial project nor a lost cause. The Nazis idealized unity in organic, biological, racializing images; the ecumenical movement insisted that real community is not natural but supernatural.

Jesus Christ, the ecumenical movement posited, is "the One who is Savior of all [hu]mankind, the Lord of Lords in whom all things hold together."[1] It acknowledged and affirmed cultural, political, and confessional differences. It insisted that we are part of a "fellowship which transcends all frontiers of nation or race or class."[2]

No one embodied this commitment to unity more than Willem Visser 't Hooft, who, as the movement institutionalized into the World Communion of Churches in 1937, became its first general secretary at the age of thirty-eight and served in this position for three decades.

For Visser 't Hooft, unity was not an ideal to strive for. Neither was it an end to be pursued through confessional or missional alignment. Rather, it was already a reality in Christ, and a gift to the church. Therefore, and only therefore, was it possible to heal divisions and overcome hostilities without falling into the temptation of uniformity.

The German Christians saw in race, folk, and nation God-given, natural orders and understood the church to be a part of these orders as well. For Visser 't Hooft, such appropriation of God for a particular culture, language, or state was thinking God too small. The Lordship of Christ would bear no such false gods next to it. Because the church's unity was not based on shared heritage or kinship, values or interests, sympathy or friendship, it could not be confined to the boundaries of ethnic, cultural, or political bodies. Nor could it be lost in the face of disagreement or even hostility.

Visser 't Hooft also vehemently resisted all those who would declare one singular issue, principle, or project so exclusively important that it justified breaking away from those with other priorities. This was reflected in the constitution of the World Council of Churches itself, which formed around several pillars, not just dialogues on Faith and Order but also on Life and Work, and on mission and evangelism.

Conversations over different interpretations of the faith, advocacy for peace and justice, service for the marginalized and poor, and proclamation of the gospel could not be in competition with each other. Their grounding in Christ meant that they should instead deepen and enrich each other.

Precisely because of their multifaceted nature, ecumenical networks became pivotal for relief and advocacy work during the height of the Third Reich. Ecumenical networks leveraged existent transnational connections, infrastructure, and moral authority; they facilitated the flow of information, aid, and refugees across borders; they provided financial aid, logistical support, and direct assistance; they directed international attention to atrocities committed, facilitated escape routes, and sheltered those fleeing from Nazi Germany for reasons far beyond religious persecution.

In a world of fragmentation and polarization, it is easy to retreat into echo chambers. In a world of hate and violence, it is understandable to seek safe and like-minded spaces. In a world of xenophobia and tribalism, it is tempting to care only about what concerns me and my own. In a world of ever-increasing complexity, it is a relief to focus on a singular goal.

Insisting on greater unity is demanding work. But it stretches the space of belonging beyond likeness and forms the capacity for disagreement beyond hostility.

Unity is not a claim that we agree on all things, or even the hope of future agreement. Unity is a commitment to grapple with one another, rather than give one another up. Unity insists that we have something to learn from each other, and that our gifts can complement each other. Unity does not mean integrating smoothly or sweeping disagreements under the rug. Unity means curating spaces in which we can challenge one another in a spirit of love.

Protect spaces of encounter.

Strengthen institutions that house complexities.

Cultivate spaces of disagreement where conflicting perspectives can enter into dialogue.

Build bridges and hold open space. Doing so does not guarantee healing and reconciliation, nor should it. But doing so makes them possible.

Because of—not in spite of—its insistence on unity, genuine ecumenism is not a passive exchange of ideas but a challenge to the way things are.

Holding onto unity means committing to mutual accountability, questioning, and learning.

Holding onto unity means not leaving anyone behind.

Holding onto unity means refusing to sacrifice individual members for the sake of the body.

A body that is fully purified will die. A heart that is fully in sync will stop beating. A living body thrives because it preserves and protects difference.

PART 4

"GO INTO THE WORLD," OR SENDING

22

"Get Thee Behind Me, Satan," *or* Get out of Yourself

There is no gathering without sending. The feeding of the crowd is nourishment for the road. The miracle of real community is a special blessing that strengthens us for everyday existence. A Sabbath between weeks of labor. Inhaling between exhales.

If we try to make it last, it loses its blessing.

If we try to immunize it against what seems unholy, it becomes cruel.

If we try to make it all-encompassing, it begets terror.

If we withdraw into it altogether, we evade our call.

The cross is a part of Christian life. As long as this earth is unredeemed, we cannot avoid it. Where we try to avoid it, we just end up putting others on it.

Jesus admonishes the disciples not to linger but to get out there: "Take up [your] cross and follow me" (Mark 8:34). When Jesus starts talking about the cross, Peter rebukes him. Maybe Peter worried that such talk would scare others off. Maybe he was hoping to avoid such a fate himself.

Maybe he was concerned that this theme was taking away from the miracle, the feeding of the crowd they had just witnessed. Whatever his intentions, Jesus recognizes the temptation and responds: "Get thee behind me, Satan" (Mark 8:33 KJV).

Six days later—the timing is no coincidence—they are once more granted respite and rest, retreat to a safe and sacred space. Away from the road, up on the mountainside, they get another taste of glory: Jesus is transfigured. Away from the road, up on the mountainside, they again experience miraculous community: not just with one another but with their forebears and exemplars of faith, Moses and Elijah. Away from the road, up on the mountainside, they are once more tempted to stay rather than to get back out there: "Rabbi, it is good for us to be here," Peter says, then pleads, "let us set up three tents: one for you, one for Moses, and one for Elijah" (Mark 9:5).

"Get thee behind me, Satan." Experiences of solitude and holy community are special blessings. Safe spaces, sacred times, and untouchable moments replenish our energies and reorient us to joy and glory. They de-normalize normality and resensitize us to challenge it. They lend us comfort and strength. But we cannot stay there.

The Christian belongs out in the world. Blessing turns into temptation when we use community to escape the world.

Get out of yourself. Confining the range of your experience to comfort and community reinforces divisions into friend and enemy. Do not believe in these divisions.

Retreating into private spaces is a form of anticipatory obedience. Do not obey.

A time of war fosters a scarcity mind-set and urges self-preservation and self-defense. Insist that blessing is not scarce; it grows when it is poured out freely.

Gather yourself in but get back out there. Refocus from the experienced blessings, to where you are being called. Turn outward from yourself to your community and from your community to the world. What are you receiving in solitude that the community needs? What are you receiving in the safety of your community that the world needs?

Crucify your desire to escape the cross.

Stay with the discomfort.

Stay with the crucified God: Stay with the crucified people.

You will not escape the cross, but you will find community right there: You are not alone.

23

"Find Power in Weakness," *or* Practice Creative Nonconformity

Václav Havel, the author and dissident who would later, as president, lead Czechoslovakia's transition into the Czech Republic, lucidly diagnosed how ideology functions. Ideology, he laid out in his famous essay *The Power of the Powerless*, forms "a bridge of excuses between the system and the individual," a "veil behind which human beings can hide their own fallen existence, their trivialization, and their adaptation to the status quo."[1]

Havel discusses the example of a greengrocer who puts a poster with a party slogan on display in his shop window. The greengrocer is not a fervent supporter of the regime. He surely is not a perpetrator of any atrocities. He is just trying to avoid an accusation of disloyalty, and the poster display seems like an innocuous enough demand to not take a personal risk.

But by displaying the poster, Havel argues, the greengrocer both signals his submission to the regime and is humiliated by it as he performs an act that is not his own. Individuals, Havel notes, "need not accept the lie. It is enough for them to have accepted their life with it and in it. For by this very fact, individuals confirm the system, fulfill the system, make the system, are the system."[2]

Compromise always leads to more compromise. It is the slow heating up of the water to boil the frog. The first step always feels small and justifiable—that's what makes it the most dangerous one.

Once in compliance, it is difficult to get out of it.

Once one has followed one order, it becomes more difficult to resist the next.

Authoritarian regimes will even make inconspicuous and small demands strategically, to gain that crucial first compliance. Many frogs will turn the dial themselves if given the opportunity, deluding themselves that they are controlling the process.

The best way to resist moral collapse is to refuse the very first step.

Hebe Kohlbrugge saw any compliance with dictatorial regimes as a fatal error. The granddaughter of a prominent nineteenth-century Dutch theologian, Hebe intentionally went into Nazi Germany to work on the ground, first with youth in the church, later as a courier between pastors in the Confessing Church, smuggling information and documents back and forth. She survived imprisonment in the infamous women's prison in Ravensbrück. And after the war, Kohlbrugge continued to work just as ardently on building networks of personal relationships with underground churches in the emerging Eastern European communist regimes.

In postwar Eastern Europe, churches at first only had to register as official institutions with the state. Once registered, they had to deliver reports on their members. Then their teaching became subject to censure. Finally, they had to align their theology and ecclesial life with state ideology.

From her experience first with the Nazi dictatorship and then with Eastern European communism, Hebe Kohlbrugge recognized the value of tactical engagement. But with moral clarity and unwavering integrity, she was deeply suspicious of anyone who thought they could avert the worst, or do more good by staying within the system.

The church's primary calling is not to survive but to be faithful, Kohlbrugge held. It is better for the church to be persecuted than to betray its calling. It must be willing to give up institutional form and standing. Out of this conviction, Kohlbrugge refused to work with officially recognized churches and intentionally sought out underground groups.

"My grace is sufficient for you, for my power is made perfect in weakness," Kohlbrugge would cite (2 Cor. 12:9). A church that chooses institutional self-preservation over prophetic witness, Kohlbrugge was convinced, is already spiritually dead. Only the church that is willing to die for its faith will truly endure.

The urge to cling to decorum, stability, and self-preservation is strongest for those who have some standing. But it will lead from compliance into compromise and moral collapse.

Don't give in to pressure.

Don't do things just because everyone does them now.

Resist conforming, especially in small and mundane things that signal nothing but your humiliation and moral submission.

Find creative ways to nonconform. Karl Barth avoided giving the expected Hitler salute to his students by starting his classes with a hymn. The greengrocer might have gotten away with losing the poster, hanging it upside down, or displaying it with a large stain of beet juice.

Maybe some of these things are not the hill you want to die on. Fair. But conformity is self-fulfilling, and nonconformity is a muscle that has to be developed and strengthened.

Find ways to build that muscle.

24

"Prepare the Ground," *or* Cultivate Relationships

Hebe Kohlbrugge practiced a different kind of ecumenicism than her Dutch compatriot Willem Visser 't Hooft. Hers was more inconspicuous but no less effective. Hers was more uncompromising but no less powerful. Where he focused on transnational institution-building and official dialogues, she was all about grassroots ecumenism.

> When a large crowd was gathering, as people were coming to [Jesus] from town after town, he said in a parable: "A sower went out to sow his seed, and as he sowed some fell on a path and was trampled on, and the birds of the air ate it up. Some fell on rock, and as it grew up it withered for lack of moisture. Some fell among thorns, and the thorns grew with it and choked it. Some fell into good soil, and when it grew it produced a hundredfold." As he said this, he called out, "If you have ears to hear, then hear!" (Luke 8:4–8)

Hebe Kohlbrugge invested in relationships and interpersonal encounter. Only through trust building and friendship, she was convinced, could understanding and solidarity be pursued. Kohlbrugge offered direct support to individuals and small groups in underground settings, visited them and communicated with them, built connections with people across denominational, national, and ideological divides all over Eastern Europe.

Her quiet and tireless, courageous and steadfast work sustained theological formation in many underground communities into which she smuggled Bibles, books, and other study materials. It encouraged those resisting state-controlled churches, and strengthened many to remain strong against co-optation by ideology. It formed networks of solidarity among persecuted believers in different countries. In the postcommunist era, many of those formed in these networks rose to become leaders of Christian communities across Europe.

Trust grows slowly. Relationship building requires personal touch as well as consistent and sustained effort. Sharing space, sharing experiences, sharing stories, sharing food, sharing memories. The farther away those with whom you build are, the more tangible and material the sharing must be.

Everything you do to build trust has to be repeated time and again to sustain it; some things daily, some things weekly, some things season by season, some things year by year.

A sower who runs through the landscape scattering seeds will waste seed and time, and reap nothing.

Don't let the seeds be trampled—use discretion where you sow them.

Don't throw the seeds on the rocks—prepare the soil.

Don't lose them under the thorns—weed out misconceptions and mistrust time and again.

Don't let the birds find them—protect the spaces of exchange, and shelter your fledgling saplings of trust.

Only diligence and persistence will pay off. Time, patience, conviviality, communication are what you have to invest. The rest is water and sunlight.

25

"Love Your Neighbor," *or* Shatter Loneliness

Our time has been characterized as the "anti-social century."[1] We have more ways than ever to be tapped into real-time conversations with people all over the globe. But the fabric of local community—villages and neighborhoods, churches and unions, kinship and interest-based networks—has disintegrated.

There are many forms of loneliness in our society, many faces of forlornness. Poverty, illness, the disembodiment of social media, remote work, hustle culture, un-, over-, and underemployment, and many other factors erode belonging, family, and community long before politics do. Polarization, fear, and worry will only exacerbate loneliness.

Combat the feelings of forlornness many already feel, and will experience even more under authoritarian conditions. Even before they need friends, everyone will need neighbors.

Those vulnerable to public exposure will withdraw, for good reason. Don't deprive them of companionship just because you cannot change their predicament.

Many relationships will rupture due to polarization and alienation, disillusionment and suspicion. You cannot effect systemic change at will. But as you can cultivate solitude and community, you can also be a neighbor to those around you.

Love your neighbor. Together with the love of God, this commandment forms the bedrock of Christian ethics. Love of neighbor is not about affection; it is about presence, care, and assistance.

"Who is my neighbor?" From the story of the Good Samaritan, we know that this is already the wrong question. We have fallen under the robbers. Jesus is the Good Samaritan. Because he becomes a neighbor to all of us, we can become neighbors to each other. In fact, it is our task to "welcome one another . . . just as Christ has welcomed [us]" (Rom. 15:7).

God's help comes to us from beyond our own powers. And we remain in need of others "as the bearers and proclaimers" of God's help, knows Bonhoeffer: "The Christ in one's own heart is weaker than the Christ in the word of other Christians."[2] It is in the neighbor that God's love is made present, manifest, and real for us.

Sometimes your neighbor will be that sibling for you. Sometimes you will be that sibling for your neighbor. Christ on the road often passes incognito. Often you might not even know when it happens. But you can reciprocate and extend neighborliness.

Being a neighbor does not depend on shared commitments, shared goals, or a shared way of life, only that you attend to those God puts in your path. Any person that shares physical space with you, on your street, at your job, at the grocery store is your neighbor—*if* you become a neighbor to them.

What makes a neighbor? Attention and listening. Practical assistance in everyday tasks. And sharing in the other's burden.

You don't have to *look* for neighbors. You have to *be* one to find them.

You don't have to *like* your neighbors. You have to be *there* for them.

Do you know your neighbors? The person living next door, your coworker down the hall, the crossing guard on your street, the secretary at your school—do you know their name? Would you know if something changed in their life? Would you notice if they withdrew or disappeared? If they were frightened or if they became radicalized? How would you spot the signs?

Be mindful of who never enters your space or your vision—kept from becoming your neighbor by walls, highways, and school districts; kept from becoming your neighbor by different timetables, routines, and patterns of movement; kept from becoming your neighbor by divisions between urban centers, suburban towns, and rural areas.

You might have relatively little in common with your neighbor. Sometimes you might even have reason to distrust them. That's okay. Even the Good Samaritan does not become a close personal friend to the person fallen under the robbers. He leaves some money to support their recovery and otherwise keeps on keeping on. He attends to their need without fuss, but also without endangering himself or losing sight of his own journey.

Make sure those around you know your face, your voice, and your name. In a climate of disconnection and fear, even eye contact and small talk might mean more to your neighbor than you can fathom. It will also alleviate your own loneliness.

Make it a standard practice to recognize and acknowledge your neighbor's humanity. It only takes a greeting and a kind word to build connection. Cultivate connections and belonging with people around you, everyday connections independent of political or ideological alignment, connections that you might need one day, connections that they might need every day.

Be attentive.

Be present.

Be kind.

Listen.

Extend assistance in mundane and everyday matters.

Share some of their burdens even when you cannot take them away.

Build networks of mutual aid and support that you want to be in place before they become necessary.

26

"Redeem the Time," *or* Delay and Prepare

"See then that ye walk circumspectly, not as fools, but as wise, redeeming the time, because the days are evil," writes the apostle Paul to the Ephesians (5:15–16 KJV). Sometimes you cannot save the world, but you can buy time. Valuable time so that some can reach safety. Valuable time to communicate and regroup. Valuable time for something or someone to get in the way. If evil seems inevitable, the least you can do is delay and deflect.

In his prison cell in Berlin-Tegel, Dietrich Bonhoeffer struggled with waves of despair and suicidal ideation. Entrusting to his closest friend what he was even unable to tell his fiancée, Maria von Wedemeyer, Bonhoeffer wrote to Eberhard Bethge: "You are the only person who knows that 'sadness' with its ominous consequences has often haunted me, and you perhaps worried about me in this respect—so I feared at the time. But I have told myself from the beginning that I will do neither human beings nor the devil this favor; if they want it done, they better finish it themselves—and I hope that I may remain steadfast in this."[1]

Bonhoeffer kept the despair at bay and did not die by his own hand. During the following year and a half of his imprisonment he would produce some of the deepest reflections and beautiful poems and hymns. His writings on the multidimensionality of life and the Christian faith in a religionless time, on the crucified God and on discipleship as standing with God in God's suffering, have since become an inspiration for many.

Bonhoeffer surely redeemed the time. If the Nazis had not executed him when their defeat became imminent, he might even have survived to see his *Ethics* to completion.

The German industrialist Oskar Schindler did not take down the Nazis. In fact, he even held a party membership, as did so many to keep their businesses running. Nor did Schindler heroically refuse when ordered to convert his enamelware factory to ammunition production. He did, however, protect about 1,200 Jews from deportation to concentration camps by insisting that they were indispensable employees in this production. By the end of the war, Schindler had spent his entire fortune on bribes to Nazi officials and support for his workers. He literally bought out the time for his employees.

French railroad workers did not dare refuse Nazis who overtook their train system for troop movements. Yet they engaged in small acts of sabotage—misrouting trains, delaying shipments, and faking equipment malfunctions. While any of these acts might seem useless, even ridiculous, the accumulated effect was a significant disruption of German logistics. It slowed the movement of troops, weapons, and supplies to the front. It disrupted the Nazi response to D-Day, giving Allies crucial time to advance. And it protected the resistance networks by framing most acts of sabotage as incompetence and bad luck.

Similarly, Danish officials blocked Nazi demands by using excessive paperwork and bureaucratic stalling tactics. In deliberate acts of administrative inefficiency, they pretended to lose files, required multiple layers of approval, and created extra paperwork. When receiving deportation orders, officials delayed by citing technical issues, asking for clarifications, requesting additional confirmation. Some did even less than that: by simply doing *Dienst nach Vorschrift*—obnoxiously insisting on following the law to the letter rather than scrambling to fulfill the demands directly—they kept themselves blameless while creating significant friction and even legal roadblocks for Nazi objectives.

All of this changed nothing about what the Nazis were doing. But it bought some time. This time was used by government and resistance movements to orchestrate the rescue of nearly all Danish Jews by ferrying them to Sweden in October 1943. Over 7,200 lives were saved.

You can only outlive the horror if you are alive. Even if you cannot see a light at the end of the tunnel, you can buy time. Time for a new day to dawn. For their evil hearts to stop beating. For the empire to crumble. For the world to end.

Staying alive matters.

Keeping others alive matters.

Redeeming the time might mean pushing papers slowly.

It might mean ignoring a knock on the door.

It might mean holding up a search until a warrant, signed by a federal judge, is produced.

Buying time might mean creating networks of support before they are needed, so that they are up and running when push comes to shove.

Buying time might mean dedicating some of your resources to creating buffers between the threats on the horizon and the bodies of those targeted.

Buying time might mean being prepared when they come for you. Have your papers in order, supplies at hand, and an emergency plan in place. Who needs to be contacted? Where will you go? Who will pick up life-sustaining duties and concerns? How will you stay in touch with those you care about and who care about you?

It takes time to meditate on these questions and put plans into place—so redeem the time. Prepare now.

27

"Come to Me . . . ," *or* Allow People to Change

Barth was an outspoken critic throughout Hitler's reign. After the military defeat of Germany sealed its moral failure, Barth was also the first to insist: What the Germans needed now, more than anything, was friends. In this their moment of utter devastation, Barth drew out Jesus's call according to Matthew 11 into an almost shocking embrace:

> Come to me, all you unpleasant ones, you evil Hitler boys and Hitler girls, you brutal SS soldiers, you horrendous Gestapo villains, you sad compromisers and collaborators, all you who followed the crowd, who for so long so patiently and stupidly followed your so-called *Führer*! Come to me, you who are guilty and complicit, and who are now experiencing and must experience what your deeds have earned! Come to me, I know you well, I do not ask you who you are and what you have done, I see only that you are at the end, and that, whether you like it or not, you must start

over, I will give you rest and refresh you, precisely with you I will now begin from scratch![1]

Forgiveness is a treacherous thing. If forgiveness is demanded or claimed outright, it puts a blanket over harm done. If it is withheld altogether, it forces perpetrator and victim to remain defined by their past. In both cases, it is the opposite of grace: It enables sin rather than overcoming it.

There is wisdom in traditional rituals of penance. They know that true "contrition of the heart" and spoken "confession of the mouth" precede any absolution given, and that receiving such forgiveness will necessarily be followed by "reparation through works of love." Without these other elements, forgiveness is not a sacrament but plain injustice.

But where it allows someone to actually become a new person, forgiveness is the gospel itself.

After the first Great War, the Treaty of Versailles forced Germany to assume the moral and financial "sole guilt" for the war. This was surely justified; Germany had unilaterally caused the aggression. But feelings of national humiliation and responsibility for heavy compensations did not create the conditions for change. They tethered Germany's future to its past, even physically, through the subsequently required reparations.

And they filled German politics with resentment and denial. Resentment and denial did not lead to repentance and conversion, but to increased hostility and aggression.

History might not repeat itself, but guilt does: first as tragedy, and then as utter horror.

Shaming and blaming make people defensive. This is well-known. It isolates and antagonizes them. It prompts them to double-down and dig in their heels. They direct anger and resentment outward instead of asking themselves hard questions.

Allow people to change.

There will be people who fall from the MAGA bandwagon. Be ready to catch them.

There will be people who start having doubts. Make space where they can voice such doubts, and embrace such doubts.

There will be people who become alienated from the authoritarian movement. Be their friend.

Friendship holds people accountable—not by guilting or shaming, not by pointing fingers and calling names, but by extending a hand that lifts up and lifts out.

Friendship holds people accountable—not by cutting off and isolating, but by furnishing relationships in which right life is possible.

Friendship integrates the sinner into human community. In this way, friendship literally sanctifies: Friendship creates the space and offers the conditions in which someone can live as a new person.

It must have been terrifying for Ananias to take the blinded Paul in. Just three days earlier, this man had been "breathing threats and murder against the disciples of the Lord" (Acts 9:1). He claimed to have seen the light. Good for him. But even if Ananias wasn't feeling vengeful, wouldn't prudence and self-preservation demand that he stay clear? Why should he go out of his way to find and take Saul in?

It must have been terrifying for Saul, lost and vulnerable, to be at the mercy of those he had previously persecuted. How easy it would have been for them to take revenge. How understandable it would have been for them to reject him and leave him out to dry. Why should they trust him? Why should he trust them?

It must have been the grace of God that made this possible. But by this grace, a remarkable act of healing happened. It gave Paul new sight, and it gave the church one of its most effective apostles.

We might not be able to work such a miracle. But we can make space for it to happen.

Spot the signs of a person who is ready to change, and allow them to become that new person.

28

"What Do You Have That You Did Not Receive?," *or* Pass on the Word

Angel is just an ancient word for messenger. Half of our New Testament is composed of letters. Its entirety is messages, passed on.

"What do you have that you did not receive?" Paul writes in a letter to Christians in Corinth (1 Cor. 4:7).

Paul writes letters. Letters to communities in Corinth and Thessaloniki, Galatia and Ephesus, and even at the heart of the empire, in faraway Rome. Paul writes letters to people he knows well, to strengthen and instruct them. Paul writes letters to people he has never met, to connect his experience with theirs.

Others also write letters, some of which are also in our canon. There are many more letters outside of our canon. These letters bridge time and distance as they remind others what they have received, and as they pass on to others what they themselves have received.

What have you that you did not receive? Many of the figures we have met in these pages wrote letters. Barth wrote thousands of letters. So did Bonhoeffer. Visser 't Hooft wrote even more. The three actually exchanged letters with one another. Hebe Kohlbrugge smuggled sermons by Martin Niemöller. The White Rose read sermons written by Bishop Galen. They distributed leaflets, citing Scripture and German literature, to their fellow students.

Whatever the medium—these messages served to clarify their thoughts, name their realities, and strengthen their resolve. They created space to exchange ideas, dream dreams, and make plans. They imparted wisdom and instruction, and allowed it to be passed on further. The Nazis considered many of these communications criminal, some even acts of treason, and people died to pass on such messages. That's how dangerous communication of insights, beliefs, and ideas was to the regime.

What do you have that you did not receive? If it were not for finding a wholly other God in Paul's letter to the Romans, Karl Barth might not have known how to distinguish the Word of God from the words of nationalism and war around him. If it were not for his experience of Black Christians in Harlem, Bonhoeffer might not have known how to talk about the crucified God. Had he not encountered the international student movement and the social gospel, Visser 't Hooft might not have known how to think about unity. If he had not been reoriented by two Roman Catholic friends from a career in medicine, Hans Scholl might not have devoted himself to the pursuit of truth and beauty. Had she not been inspired by iconic poets and philosophers, Sophie Scholl might not have had the courage to denounce the atrocities of the Third Reich.

What do you have that you did not receive? We have all received grace upon grace from others. Be on the lookout to find more.

Rest assured that very little is actually unprecedented under the sun. There is a great cloud of witnesses that has come before you. There is a great cloud of witnesses even today, in many places.

Connect with them. Get access to their experience.

Educate yourself and read widely.

Let yourself be inspired by art and music.

Study, investigate, and research to gain depth.

Learn from those far away and long ago. Learn to recognize similarities and differences. Learn from movements of resistance that have been successful, and even more from those that have failed. Learn from the ecumenical church and communities around the globe. Learn from those in other traditions of faith, and in other political trajectories.

Reflect. Apply. Synthesize.

Discuss with others.

Rearticulate. Communicate. Create.

Know that you're not alone and let others know that they are not alone, either. Preserve the wisdom and insight you have received, and pass on your own. Maybe you, too, want to write a letter or two? Maybe you, too, want to become a messenger?

Paul tells the Christians in Corinth, "You yourselves

are our letter, written on our hearts, known and read by all, and you show that you are a letter of Christ, prepared by us, written not with ink but with the Spirit of the living God, not on tablets of stone but on tablets that are human hearts" (2 Cor. 3:2–3).

Conclusion

"Build Houses . . . ," *or* Transform Your Hope

"The grass withers; the flower fades," sings the prophet Isaiah, "but the word of our God will stand forever" (40:8). Both prophet and teacher know: This, too, will end. Neither power nor wealth lasts forever. Kingdoms crumble. Empires fall. The sun rises, and the sun goes down. The wind blows to the south and goes around to the north. A crack in the concrete. A new generation is born.

Unprecedented. I cannot count how often I have heard this word during the past years. The constant state of exception, people keep saying, has become a "new normal." Maybe such is to be expected at the "end of the world"—a trope that is also often invoked these days. And yet, as every turn seems even more dramatic than before, that, too, is starting to feel familiar.

I remember being taught about the Ottoman Empire in grade school. I laughed when I saw that the period marked as "decline" extended over three hundred years. Surely that was not "decline" but simply "history"? The decline and fall of the Roman Empire even took a millennium and a half, and in some ways, we might still be living through its ripples.[1]

Some empires fall rapidly, but most are slowly hollowed out from the inside and weakened from the outside before they ultimately collapse. Hollywood wants us to believe that the end of the world is one big, urgent, catastrophic doomsday.

But more likely, it looks like this: the fizzling out of a world power on rising tides, further destabilized by infighting and scapegoating, while everyone scrambles for pieces of a pie that suddenly seems up for grabs, even as it is now also perceptibly shrinking. The orchestra continues to play while the ship is sinking, first imperceptibly and slowly, then drastically and chaotically, eventually collapsing altogether into the sea. Some of the ripples go halfway across the world. But the ocean is good at keeping secrets.

The rise of authoritarianism is part of the implosion of an empire. As systemic crises escalate, as control slips from grip, the fist tightens, grasping at straws on the road of inevitable decline.

We might stop this wave of authoritarianism.

We might rebuild some semblance of democracy and social order. I hope we will.

Even so, the world we are inhabiting is collapsing. Authoritarianism is a symptom of the crisis, not its singular cause.

Have you not known? Have you not heard?
    Has it not been told you from the beginning?
    Have you not understood from the foundations
        of the earth?
It is he who sits above the circle of the earth,
    and its inhabitants are like grasshoppers,
who stretches out the heavens like a curtain
    and spreads them like a tent to live in,
who brings princes to naught
    and makes the rulers of the earth as nothing.
        (Isa. 40:21–23)

We've been here before.

This is not the first end of the world. Many worlds have ended.

This is also not the first time that people have falsely placed their faith, their love, and their hope in an empire, its prowess and economic force, its ability to bring about some measure of justice, peace, and flourishing, or to restore law, order, and decency.

In times of collapse, believers scramble to disentangle their faith in God from such misplaced belief. In a remarkable book about current changes in the social order, theologian Ted Smith calls this process "renunciation."[2] While such moments are full of anguish and grief, and often tremendous suffering, they have also offered remarkable new insights, turns, and liberations. Smith calls these "affordances."

Five hundred years ago, Martin Luther was deadly afraid that the "Turks before Vienna" were God's judgment: "unbelievers" sent by God to destroy the decadent Holy Roman Empire of the German nation. And yet, asked what he would do if tomorrow the world ended, Luther responded: "Then today, I would plant an apple tree."[3]

Hope invests in timelines beyond our individual life when catastrophe cannot be averted. Luther's insistent critique of the Roman Church and his renewed emphasis on God's grace were part of the Reformation. This movement was precipitated by a period of crisis in the empire marked by great economic hardship and social unrest, technological innovation and international trade leading to the rise of urban elites, weakening imperial rule and power shifts to regional dynasties. External threats by competitor empires like the Ottomans and the conquest of the Americas further "widened" the world and shook up its order.

The religious fragmentation of the Reformation was an expression of these crises and deepened them further. Then, it also became a major factor in its institutional and structural transformation. This transformation eventually enabled the empire to endure several hundred years more, until its dissolution under Napoleon.

Like the successor Holy Roman Empire of Luther's time, the Nazis, too, saw themselves as heirs of the first Roman Empire—hence, they called theirs the *Third* Reich. For many, Nazi Germany shattered the idols of modernity, as the dreams of liberty, justice, and brotherhood of all mankind result not in cosmopolitan pluralism and world peace but in technocratic totalitarianism, a war the like of which the earth had not yet known, and the genocide of God's chosen people.

The question "Where was God at Auschwitz?" marked perhaps the biggest crisis of the Christian faith since the demise of the first Roman Empire. The numbers of the Nazis' victims and the highly organized manner of their execution are unfathomable.

The Nazis aspirationally called their reign of terror the "Thousand Year Reich." It ended after twelve.

Yet the idols appear persistent, their promises great.

Apparently, they still need to be shattered, today.

Both of these successors pointed back to the Roman Empire. When the same empire that had crucified Jesus and persecuted Christians elevated Christianity into its official religion under Constantine, many saw the realization of God's kingdom on earth manifested in imperial peace. While others remained more cautious about the fusion between divine authority and political rule, when Rome was sacked in 410, Christian political theology lay in shambles. How could the earthly manifestation of God's kingdom possibly *end*?

Not only were their own imperial hopes destroyed, Christians were also blamed by their contemporaries, accused of having weakened and emasculated the reign. In the biggest transformation of Christian hope since the delayed coming-again of Jesus, Augustine of Hippo wrote the *City of God*, in which he proclaimed that the fall of Rome was not the end of Christian hope but rather the inevitable decline of worldly power in the cycles of history. He emphatically desacralized political power and alerted Christians to the ongoing presence of God's kingdom in their hearts. He emphasized the need to strive for spiritual transformation while participating boldly and fully in the world.

Even more devastating than any Roman kingdom's fall must have been the fall of Jerusalem under Nebuchadnezzar. The land God had promised to Israel was taken away and occupied, the Holy City and even the temple, the holiest of holies, destroyed and desecrated, the people of God exiled to Babylon.

It ought to have been the end of this faith, the end of all hope.

And yet, the prophet Jeremiah writes to those in exile—another letter, full of wisdom, full of hope. Denying none of their suffering, he urges them to transform their hope and redirects them to the here and now: "Build houses and live in them; plant gardens and eat what they produce. Take wives and have sons and daughters; take wives for your sons, and give your daughters in marriage, that they may bear sons and daughters; multiply there, and do not decrease. But seek the welfare of the city where I have sent you into exile, and pray to the LORD on its behalf, for in its welfare you will find your welfare" (Jer. 29:5–7).

The end of the world was not the end of Israel. The miracle happened: Israel's hope was transformed, from one built on territorial possession, religious centralization, and a royal dynasty into a hope that comes to life until today in the study of scriptures, resounds in a network of synagogues, and expanded their witness to the power of God into all the world.

Today's end of the world demands a similar transformation of Christian hope. It demands a transformation of Christian life and praxis. This demand is simply the unfinished business begun by the carpenter's shout in Galilee: "The kingdom of God has come near; repent, and believe in the good news" (Mark 1:15).

Some of his closest disciples hoped this carpenter would gather the twelve tribes once more, lead the insurrection to overthrow the Romans and restore the political kingdom of Israel. They were sorely disappointed.

For many, all hope ended when Jesus died at that cross; others would soon reinvest their hope into the empire that crucified him.

But to some, a risen Christ appeared, broke bread, and stayed a while.

They did not recognize him at first. First, their hope had to be transformed.

"See, I am making all things new . . ." (Rev. 21:5).

The end has already come. Our hope cannot remain tethered to the conditions that sustained it for so long that we started to mistake these conditions for our hope. It must be transformed.

None of this is unprecedented; what is unprecedented is that today it is we who have to do the hard work of seeing idols smashed, grieving and picking up the pieces, holding them up to the sun, and seeing new refractions of light in their edges.

Where does this fit? What work might it yet do?

How does one confess one's faith, not in one act that ends it all but in the on-going-ness of this ending?

How will you live in "such a time as this"?

First Aid Kit

If you are looking for **priorities**, go to lesson 9.

If you feel **overwhelmed**, go to lessons 1, 2, and 16.

If you feel **isolated**, go to lessons 7, 20, 25, and 28.

If you are looking for **discernment**, go to lessons 3, 4, 5, 12, 13, and 20.

If you are looking for **understanding**, go to lessons 3, 8, 12, 13, 14, and 23.

If you are looking for **self-examination**, go to lessons 3, 5, and 6.

If you are looking for **encouragement**, go to lessons 6, 10, and 22.

If you are looking to **ground yourself in what is good**, go to lessons 15 and 17.

If you are looking for **spiritual practices**, go to lessons 15, 16, 17, 18, and 19.

If you want to **snap into action**, go to lessons 9, 10, 11, 12, 14, and 22.

If you are looking to **steel your resolve**, go to lessons 9, 10, 11, 12, 14, 19, 22, and 23.

If you are **working in community**, go to lessons 17, 18, 20, 21, 24, 25, 27, and 28.

If you are **working in institutions**, go to lessons 5, 7, 11, 19, 20, 21, and 28.

If you are **impatient with those around you**, go to lessons 7, 17, 20, 21, and 27.

If you feel **powerless or insufficient**, go to lessons 2, 5, 7, 20, and 25.

If you are looking for **patience**, go to lessons 6, 19, 24, and 26.

If the **work feels heavy**, go to lessons 5, 9, and 15.

If you **don't know where to start**, go to lesson 5.

Study Guide

For each lesson, I have compiled some questions for self-examination, reflection, and discussion, and some suggestions for practical and concrete actions. Feel free to draw on them, but feel even freer to come up with questions and actions that seem more pertinent for your context and community. For each lesson, I also list resources that will allow you to dig deeper into history, theology, and guidance for action.

Introduction
"There Is Nothing New Under the Sun," *or* We've Been Here Before

Reflect

How would you describe these times? What scares you? What gives you hope?

What experiences and histories, stories and images from your community can illuminate these times?

What resources do you have to bring to the table for wisdom and guidance?

Try this

Discuss your perception of these times with others.

Revisit sources of wisdom and insight and deepen your understanding of them.

Share and compare with others.

Dig deeper

Wolfgang Benz, Thomas Dunlap, and Susanne Simor. *A Concise History of the Third Reich*. University of California Press, 2007.

Anne Applebaum. *Twilight of Democracy: The Seductive Lure of Authoritarianism*. Vintage Books, 2021.

Timothy Snyder. *The Road to Unfreedom: Russia, Europe, America*. Crown, 2019.

Masha Gessen. *Surviving Autocracy*. Riverhead Books, 2020.

Jason Stanley. *How Fascism Works*. Random House, 2020.

1
"He Then Rebuked the Wind . . . ," *or* Find Calm

Reflect

Have you recently experienced emotional "flooding"? What triggered it? What helped you? What could you do to prepare yourself for or protect yourself from similar situations in the future?

To whom and to what—relationships, goals, values, commitments—do you *want* to give your attention? What can you do to ensure you have attention for who and what matters most to you?

Try this

Take five minutes to write out what overwhelms you, what distresses you, what makes you anxious. No self-censoring; put it all on paper. Then light a candle and burn the paper. Sit with the candle for five more minutes and breathe.

Set specific times during which you catch up on news, and keep other times free from the news.

Formulate NMWs ("no matter what's")—habits, commitments, relationships—to which you want to devote your attention no matter what else is going on. Set aside times (at the beginning or end of your day, at specific times during the week, or every time you brush your teeth / walk the dog / fuel the car, etc.) to ensure you can attend to them.

Dig deeper

Karl Barth. *Theological Existence To-Day! A Plea for Theological Freedom*. Translated by R. Birch Hoyle. 1934. Reprint, Wipf & Stock, 2012.

Christiane Tietz. *Karl Barth: A Life in Conflict*. Translated by Victoria Barnett. Oxford University Press, 2021.

Naomi Klein. *The Shock Doctrine: The Rise of Disaster Capitalism*. Picador, 2008.

Ezra Klein. "Don't Believe Him." *New York Times*, February 2, 2025. https://tinyurl.com/6xtmpadn.

Audre Lorde. "The Transformation of Silence into Language and Action." In *Sister Outsider: Essays and Speeches*. Penguin Books, 2020.

2
"And Jesus Wept," *or* Feel Your Feelings

Reflect

Which feelings do you feel most prominently? Where do they sit in your body? How is your body communicating them to you?

Which feelings are you uncomfortable with? Which feelings are you tempted to avoid or push aside? Why do you think that is?

Try this

Lie down or sit down in a relaxed and quiet space, inside or outside. Close your eyes. Feel your body. Feel the air expanding your lungs, the air surrounding you, the ground supporting you. Scan your body, slowly. Where do you feel tension? Release it. Invite your feelings in. Welcome them, one by one; don't judge them, don't try to think through them, just sit with them.

Put together a music playlist for a full range of emotions. Allow yourself to browse it every now and then and put on songs that you find yourself resonating with. Use the music to lean into individual emotions, to shout, run, or dance them out, on repeat, as needed.

Dig deeper

Viktor Frankl. *Man's Search for Meaning*. Beacon, 2006.

Bessel van der Kolk. *The Body Keeps the Score: Brain, Mind, and Body in the Healing of Trauma*. Penguin Books, 2015.

Audre Lorde. "The Uses of Anger: Women Responding to Racism." In *Sister Outsider: Essays and Speeches*. Penguin Books, 2020.

Arthur C. Brooks and Oprah Winfrey. *Build the Life You Want: The Art and Science of Getting Happier*. Portfolio, 2023.

3
"Deprive Them of Their Pathos," *or* Test Your Feelings

Reflect

As you feel your feelings, ask them about their names and back story. Some feelings disguise themselves as other feelings: Which part of this grief is guilt? How much of your outrage is envy? Is your anger just thinly veiled helplessness?

What journey does this feeling want to take you on? Ask yourself, what is it you want to do *because* of this feeling? Then ask yourself, what do you want to do *with* this feeling? Which response or action appeals to you? Why do you think that is? Are there other uses to which you could put this feeling? Why do you prefer one over the other?

Try this

Start an emotion journal. When you feel overwhelmed by your feelings, write down how you feel. As you do so, try to tease apart "I feel . . ." from "I think . . ." and "I want to . . ."

Dig deeper

Angela Dienhart Hancock. *Karl Barth's Emergency Homiletic, 1932–1933: A Summons to Prophetic Witness at the Dawn of the Third Reich*. Eerdmans, 2013.

Ute Frevert. *The Power of Emotions: A History of Germany from 1900 to the Present*. Cambridge University Press, 2023.

Peter Fritzsche. *Germans into Nazis*. Harvard University Press, 1999.

Robert Wuthnow. *The Left Behind*. Princeton University Press, 2019.

Jeff Sharlet. *The Undertow: Scenes from a Slow Civil War*. Norton, 2023.

Arlie R. Hochschild. *Stolen Pride: Loss, Shame, and the Rise of the Right*. New Press, 2024.

4
"Test the Spirits," *or* Practice Discernment

Reflect

Where do you turn to discern truth from falsehood? Which sources and practices do you trust?

Where do you see communal discernment happening? How can you strengthen it?

Where do you see disregard for truth? Where do you see falsehood posing for truth, or truth turned into its opposite? How do you deal with that?

Try this

Follow one local, one national, and one international news outlet.

Compare three different news channels or commentators over the course of a week. How do they differ in general? How do they differ on particular issues? Why do you think that is? How would someone see the world who only followed one of them?

Dig deeper

Doris L. Bergen. *The Twisted Cross: The German Christian Movement in the Third Reich*. University of North Carolina Press, 1996.

Claudia Koonz. *The Nazi Conscience*. Belknap Press of Harvard University Press, 2005.

Thomas Kühne. *Belonging and Genocide: Hitler's Community, 1918–1945*. Yale University Press, 2013.

Kristin Kobes du Mez. *Jesus and John Wayne: How White Evangelicals Corrupted a Faith and Fractured a Nation*. Liveright, 2021.

Matthew D. Taylor. *The Violent Take It by Force: The Christian Movement That Is Threatening Our Democracy*. Broadleaf, 2024.

5
"Wait for the Lord," *or* Confess and Recommit

Reflect

What responses to the current crises have you heard from other Christians? Why do you think they respond that way?

What responses have you given, in thought and word, in action and inaction? Why do you think you are responding in this way?

Which responses have struck you as misguided, and why? Which have you found helpful, and how?

Try this

Write a confession of sin, for you individually or for a community of which you are part (church, movement, social group, political party, etc.). Where have you dreamed dreams of greatness and exceptionalism? Where have you confused certain cultural formations with faith commitments, and certain political hopes with the kingdom of God? Where and how have you failed to attend to material injustices and to listen to people who felt increasingly abandoned and precarious? Where are you continuing to dream such dreams, indulge such confusions, and overlook injustices, even and especially in your response to the present moment?

Write a confession of faith. Who is God? What is God like? What reassurance can you draw from this truth? What does it mean to commit yourself to this God? What will it demand practically?

Dig deeper

Victoria Barnett. *"After Ten Years": Dietrich Bonhoeffer and Our Times*. Fortress, 2017.

Karl Jaspers. *The Question of German Guilt*. Translated by E. B. Ashton. Fordham University Press, 2001.

Theodor W. Adorno. *Guilt and Defense: On the Legacies of National Socialism in Postwar Germany*. Edited, translated, and introduced by Jeffrey K. Olick and Andrew J. Perrin. Harvard University Press, 2010.

Matthew D. Hockenos. *A Church Divided: German Protestants Confront the Nazi Past*. Indiana University Press, 2004.

Claudio Carvalhaes. *Liturgies from Below: Praying with People at the End of the World*. Abingdon, 2020.

6
"Faith, Hope, and Love Remain," *or* Find Purpose

Reflect

What would you keep doing even if there was no hope for success or improvement? What do you believe in against all odds? Which relationships give your actions meaning? What commitments ground you when you are not optimistic? What values are worth embodying even when no one else embodies them? Where do you find purpose in something larger than yourself? What energizes you or gives you a sense of fulfillment? What activities have you sustained through challenges or hardships?

Where are you already part of something larger than yourself? How do your interests, actions, and passions create meaning, use, and joy for yourself and others?

Where do you experience labor, pain, and suffering that you find pointless? Where do you experience labor, pain, and suffering that you find meaningful? What makes the difference?

Try this

Join a club, group, or network on the basis of an interest or commitment of yours and build relationships with others who share it with you.

Create something beautiful, something that gives you and others joy and delight.

Create something that is useful for yourself and others.

Dig deeper

Viktor Frankl. *Man's Search for Meaning*. Beacon, 2006.

Jürgen Moltmann. *Theology of Hope: On the Ground and the Implications of a Christian Eschatology*. Fortress, 1993.

James F. Keenan. *Virtues for Ordinary Christians*. Sheed & Ward, 1996.

Mariame Kaba. *We Do This 'Til We Free Us: Abolitionist Organizing and Transforming Justice*. Haymarket, 2021.

7
"Two Are Better Than One," *or* Build with What Is There

Reflect

Where have you been tempted to start from scratch, and why?

Examine dissatisfaction with an existing institution, group, or space. What puts you off, and why? Where can you compromise? Where not? Why not?

What institutions, networks, and resources do you know that might be resources in these times? Where and how might you offer them support or work with them?

Try this

Identify one institution in your context that you can befriend, and befriend it.

Dig deeper

Eberhard Busch. *The Barmen Theses Then and Now: The 2004 Warfield Lectures at Princeton Theological Seminary*. Eerdmans, 2010.

Eric Martin. *The Writing on the Wall: Signs of Faith Against Fascism*. Cascade, 2023.

Aaron Schutz and Marie G. Sandy. *Collective Action for Social Change: An Introduction to Community Organizing*. Palgrave Macmillan, 2012.

Jane F. McAlevey. *No Shortcuts: Organizing for Power in the New Gilded Age*. Oxford University Press, 2016.

8
"In the Beginning Was the Word," *or* Mind the Power of Language

Reflect

Where have you noticed changes in language? Are there particular words that have fallen into disrepute or become very fashionable? To whom and what do they get applied? What does this wording *do*?

Where do you notice language that obfuscates rather than clarifies? Where do you notice debasing and dehumanizing language? To whom does it get applied?

Where do you see slogans simplifying reality? How would you characterize in your own words what you see happening?

What might it mean to speak the truth out of responsibility

for reality rather than to destroy it? What kind of discernment, commitment, and practice does it require?

Try this

Practice translation work. Read news headlines and translate them three different ways. Why do you think the headlines were chosen as they were?

Train the following truth-speaking practice: Hold up a mirror to people you disagree with. When you hear someone talking in a way that worries you, translate what you hear into what this might mean, do, or result in. Rather than arguing or pushing back directly, ask, "I hear you say . . . This sounds like you . . . Is this what you mean?" Allow them to correct your representation, or to correct themselves. What happens next?

Support local libraries and familiarize yourself with their programming.

Dig deeper

Victor Klemperer, *The Language of the Third Reich*. Bloomsbury, 2013.

George Orwell, *Nineteen Eighty-Four*. Buccaneer, 1949.

Peter Pomerantsev. *This Is Not Propaganda: Adventures in the War Against Reality*. Faber & Faber, 2020.

Andie Tucher. *Not Exactly Lying: Fake News and Journalism in American History*. Columbia University Press, 2022.

Peter Pomerantsev. *How to Win an Information War: The Propagandist Who Outwitted Hitler*. PublicAffairs, 2024.

9

"Stand Where God Stands," *or* Protect the Weak

Reflect

Where do you feel vulnerable, exposed, and targeted in these times? Who else is similarly affected that you can connect with? Who can you see standing with you, and how?

Who is most vulnerable to persecution and repression in these times? Who is being most directly targeted? Who is left out to dry as others protect themselves?

What is your relationship to these groups? Where and how do your lives already intersect? What is one way you can shield and support them?

Try this

Call your senators and representatives when political measures target the vulnerable.

Identify an organization that protects particular vulnerable communities and schedule a recurrent payment to them, however small. Regular donations are more important than onetime support for ongoing functioning.

Many organizations and initiatives rely on volunteer support. Give your time and effort to a law clinic for immigrants, a suicide prevention hotline, a soup kitchen, a reproductive rights center, a youth group, or a local library that runs educational programs. Pick a mission that matches your skill set, time, and interests.

Dig deeper

Dietrich Bonhoeffer. *Discipleship*. Edited by Geffrey B. Kelly and John D. Godsey. Translated by Barbara Green and Reinhard Krauss. Dietrich Bonhoeffer Works (DBW) 4. Fortress, 2015.

Reggie L. Williams. *Bonhoeffer's Black Jesus: Harlem Renaissance Theology and an Ethic of Resistance*. Baylor University Press, 2014.

The Confession of Belhar. Faith Alive Christian Resources, 1986.

Gustavo Gutiérrez. *A Theology of Liberation: History, Politics, and Salvation*. Translated by Caridad Inda and John Eagleson. Orbis Books, 2023.

Sang Hyun Lee. *From a Liminal Place: An Asian American Theology*. Fortress, 2010.

10
"Stand Firm," *or* Don't Give Up Space

Reflect

In which spaces do you feel increasingly uncomfortable? Why? Who else is there, comfortable or also uncomfortable, and why? How do you want to relate to them?

In which spaces do you feel safe and secure? Why? What makes the difference? Who is in these spaces with you? How can you strengthen this space? Who is not in these spaces?

Over which spaces do you feel a degree of control or influence? How so?

Try this

Take fuller control over your space by decorating it, caring for it, signaling it.

In one space of discomfort, take a little more control: by the way you occupy it, by the way you move and speak in it, by the way you relate to others in it.

In one space of discomfort, take an action to create friction for those who feel too comfortable in it.

Dig deeper

Karl Barth. "Letter to Dietrich Bonhoeffer." In *London: 1933–1935*, edited by Keith Clements, translated by Isabel Best. DBW 13. Fortress, 2007.

Karl Barth. "Letter to a Pastor in the German Democratic Republic." In *Karl Barth and Dietrich Bonhoeffer: Theologians for a Post-Christian World*, edited by Wolf Krötke, translated by John P. Burgess. Baker Academic, 2019.

Matthew D. Hockenos. *Then They Came for Me: Martin Niemöller, the Pastor Who Defied the Nazis*. Basic Books, 2018.

Erica Chenoweth. *Civil Resistance: What Everyone Needs to Know*. Oxford University Press, 2021.

George Lakey. *How We Win: A Guide to Nonviolent Direct Action Campaigning*. Melville House, 2018.

11

"For Such a Time as This," *or* Use Your Privilege

Reflect

What privilege and power do you have? Think about your identity and social location; your skills and physical abilities; your experience, training, and credentials; your biography, family, and friends; your position, platform, and influence. Think about the spaces, communities, and institutions through which you move. What access, knowledge, and agency do they give you? To which uses can you put your freedom and options?

Where do you see dangers and threats to your integrity? Which decisions do you find imposed on you? Where do you have to make choices, and which choices do you have?

How will you adjudicate between access and agency on one hand and integrity and freedom on the other? How will you adjudicate between self-preservation and compromise?

Try this

Choose one concrete way that your position and access can be leveraged for the good of others, and exercise that leverage.

Formulate red lines you will not cross to preserve your privilege. Write them down. Share them with someone you trust to increase accountability.

Dig deeper

Dietrich Bonhoeffer. *Ethics*. Edited by Clifford J. Green. Translated by Reinhard Krauss, Charles C. West, and Douglas W. Scott. DBW 6. Fortress, 2005.

Daniel Utrecht. *The Lion of Münster: The Bishop Who Roared Against the Nazis*. TAN Books, 2016.

Michael Mueller. *Canaris: The Life and Death of Hitler's Spymaster*. Frontline Books, 2017.

Fritz Stern and Elisabeth Sifton. *No Ordinary Men: Dietrich Bonhoeffer and Hans von Dohnanyi, Resisters Against Hitler in Church and State*. New York Review Books, 2013.

Richard Selzer. *Letters to a Young Doctor*. Harcourt, Brace, 1996.

12

"Obey God More Than Humans," *or* Draw Lines

Reflect

Where have you seen individuals or institutions surrender power freely and unnecessarily? Why do you think they did? What was the effect? What could they have done differently?

Where do you feel the urge to comply with expectations before they become commands, to act on threats before they manifest? What criteria might you employ to discern between prudence and anticipatory obedience?

What are nonnegotiable lines for you? How would you act if commanded to cross them?

Try this

Write a letter to yourself laying out your values and commitments. Revisit it intermittently. If you see changes, ask yourself: Are your values developing? Or are you shifting away from them?

Imagine explicit or implicit demands that might be placed by your employer, the community, the state. Decide how you would handle them, or role-play different scenarios with friends. Make a plan for how to handle potential consequences for you and those around you.

Talk to your friends and family about the risks involved with your nonnegotiable lines.

Dig deeper

Eric Vuillard. *The Order of the Day*. Translated by Mark Polizzotti. Other Press, 2020.

Timothy Snyder. *On Tyranny*. Crown, 2017.

Stanley Milgram. *Obedience to Authority: An Experimental View*. Harper, 2009.

Reinhold Niebuhr. *Moral Man and Immoral Society: A Study in Ethics and Politics*. Must Have Books, 2021.

13
"Be Wise as Serpents and Innocent as Doves," *or* Choose Your Battles and Avoid Traps

Reflect

What are commitments for which you are ready to expose yourself? How can you minimize the risks of this exposure?

What are traps that you recognize? How can you avoid them?

How can you communicate, organize, and signal with discretion between who you want to reach and who does not need to know?

Try this

Minimize your digital footprint. Regularly audit and scrub personal information from social media, data brokers, search engines.

Lock down your devices. If your phone or laptop was seized right now, what would someone find on it?

Familiarize yourself with the data policy and privacy settings of your social media accounts, email providers, and data repositories.

Set up various lists of encrypted messengers for specific aspects of your life. Share events and information, thoughts and feelings with discretion with persons on these lists rather than on social media.

Install a VPN client.

Avoid actions that bait you into illegal behavior or proximity to police surveillance, unless you are convinced the risk is worth it. Use secure channels for organizing, work with people you trust. Assume everything you post is being watched. Know your rights.

Dig deeper

Cal Newport. *Digital Minimalism*. Portfolio, 2019.
Sun Tzu. *The Art of War*. Filiquarian, 2007.
Saul D. Alinsky. *Rules for Radicals*. Vintage Books, 1989.
Andrew Boyd and Dave Oswald Mitchell, eds. *Beautiful Trouble: A Toolbox for Revolution*. OR Books, 2012.

14
"Do Something Brave," *or* Make a Start

Reflect

Have you experienced a situation when someone should have said something? How did that make you feel? What could have gone differently, and how?

Have you experienced a situation in which you have spoken out, said no, intervened? What was the result? What conclusions did you draw? How do you feel about it now?

Where do you feel speaking out is demanded today? Who do you see speaking out? How could you use your voice?

Try this

Make it a habit to ask "why?," "really?," and "what are the other options?"

Play-act situations in which you want to speak out or intervene, ahead of time with people you trust. Practice what you'll say and do, how you'll move, react, and respond.

Get self-defense training to overcome freeze-or-flight reflexes.

Get bystander intervention training to learn the many ways to become active in scary, uncomfortable, and threatening situations.

Dig deeper

Victoria Barnett. *Bystanders: Conscience and Complicity During the Holocaust*. Praeger, 2000.

Paul Lazarsfeld, Bernard Berelson, and Hazel Gaudet. *The People's Choice: How the Voter Makes Up His Mind in a Presidential Campaign*. Columbia University Press, 2021.

Inge Scholl. *The White Rose*. Translated by Arthur R. Schultz. Wesleyan University Press, 1983.

Catherine Sanderson. *The Bystander Effect: The Psychology of Courage and How to Be Brave.* Collins, 2021.

Mariann Edgar Budde. *How We Learn to Be Brave: Decisive Moments in Life and Faith.* Avery, 2023.

15
"Rejoice Always," *or* Lean into Joy

Reflect

What fuels your joy? Where do glory and gratitude break through gloom and suffering in your life?

Do you remember occasions when you found other people's joy contagious? Do you remember occasions when you found other people's gloom contagious?

Have you experienced times when you were unable to feel joy, or appreciate it? Why do you think that was? What did it do to you? What happened then?

Try this

Go on a nature walk and pay attention to life spans that are much shorter or much longer than yours. What do insects and trees have to teach you?

When catching up with friends, make it a habit of asking them about a recent joy or delight. Share one of your own in return.

Dig deeper

Etty Hillesum. *An Interrupted Life: The Diaries of Etty Hillesum, 1941–1943*. Translated by Arnold J. Pomerans. Pantheon, 1996.

Trina Paulus. *Hope for the Flowers*. Paulist, 1973.

Octavia Butler. *Parable of the Sower*. Seven Stories, 2017.

David Brooks. "How to Stay Sane in Brutalizing Times." *New York Times*, November 2, 2023. https://tinyurl.com/5n8kj7ap.

Ross Gay. *Inciting Joy*. Algonquin Books, 2022.

adrienne maree brown. *Pleasure Activism: The Politics of Feeling Good*. AK Press, 2019.

16
"Pray Without Ceasing," *or* Fortify Interiority

Reflect

Reflect on Arendt's distinction between solitude and loneliness. Do you find the distinction clear? Recount experiences that speak to one or the other, or that blur the boundary.

Reflect on Bonhoeffer's quote about community and solitude. Are there times when you have sought solitude because you felt uncomfortable among other people, or times when you sought community because you felt uncomfortable being alone? What happened? What might be good ways to manage your feelings?

Is prayer for you a form of solitude or a form of community? Why and how so?

Try this

Befriend yourself. Invite yourself to a shared time of silence, conversation, or reflection. As you check in with yourself, treat yourself with hospitality, curiosity, and empathy.

Strengthen a spiritual practice that works for you: centering prayer, daily examen, nature walks, running, journaling, etc.

Dig deeper

Hannah Arendt. *The Origins of Totalitarianism*. Penguin, 2017.

Dietrich Bonhoeffer. *Life Together*. Translated by Daniel W. Bloesch. DBW 5. Fortress, 2015.

Dorothee Sölle. *The Silent Cry: Mysticism and Resistance*. Translated by Barbara Rumscheidt and Martin Rumscheidt. Fortress, 2001.

Henri Nouwen. *The Way of the Heart: Connecting with God Through Prayer, Wisdom, & Silence*. Ballantine Books, 2003.

Abraham Joshua Heschel. *The Sabbath*. Farrar, Straus & Giroux, 2005.

17
"Break Bread," or Nourish Community

Reflect

Have you ever experienced amazing forms of community that felt life-giving and transformative? What were they based on? How did they come about? How long did they last? What did you take with you?

Have you ever experienced a breach or betrayal of community? What happened to the community as a result? Why?

Have you ever experienced a community fracture under its ideals? What could have been done to avoid that?

Try this

Invite a group of close friends over for dinner. Then make it a weekly thing.

Identify people that are important to you, but far away. Make it a regular habit to communicate with them—whether via text messages, phone calls, or in another manner.

Express gratitude for what individual people bring to your life and community. Be specific. Do so often.

Dig deeper

Dietrich Bonhoeffer. *Life Together*. Translated by Daniel W. Bloesch. DBW 5. Fortress, 2015.

Marva J. Dawn. *Truly the Community: Romans 12 and How to Be the Church*. Eerdmans, 1997.

Willie Jennings. *Acts*. Interpretation: A Bible Commentary for Teaching and Preaching. Westminster John Knox, 2017.

bell hooks. *All About Love: New Visions*. William Morrow, 2001.

Charles Marsh. *The Beloved Community*. Basic Books, 2006.

18

"Do This in Remembrance of Me," *or* Rehearse Dangerous Memories

Reflect

What stories did you grow up with? What stories are being told in your family, community, circles of friends? What communal fabric do they weave?

Which absences weigh heavy on your present? What feelings are laden into them? What can you do to keep their memory alive?

What practices of recollection exist in your community that are not primarily narrative? Where and how do absences of recollection become present, and to what effect? Buildings and policies, images and statues—who and what do they memorialize, and how?

Try this

Take an inventory of visual and physical reminders of pasts and absences in your space. Are these the memories you want to keep alive? Make choices and changes according to your conclusions.

Light a candle for someone you worry or care about.

Make a point of telling someone else about them.

Dig deeper

Michael Welker. *What Happens in Holy Communion?* Translated by John F. Hoffmeyer. Eerdmans, 2000.

Johann Baptist Metz. *Faith in History and Society: Toward a Practical Fundamental Theology*. Translated by J. Matthew Ashley. Crossroad, 2007.

Avishai Margalit. *The Ethics of Memory*. Harvard University Press, 2002.

Rebecca Solnit. *Hope in the Dark: Untold Histories, Wild Possibilities*. Haymarket Books, 2016.

Kelly Brown Douglas. *Resurrection Hope: A Future Where Black Lives Matter.* Orbis Books, 2021.

Jason Stanley. *Erasing History: How Fascists Rewrite the Past to Control the Future.* Atria / One Signal, 2024.

19
"When Your Children Ask You . . . ," *or* Be a Little Conservative

Reflect

Find children's stories—books, shows, movies, songs—that address difficult issues in a way that is not reductive or belittling. If you can't find them, write them.

Remember your own childhood. Were there any adults who took your worries and questions seriously? How so? How did they talk to you?

On which roots are you drawing strength, and what are you working to preserve?

What is the meaning of the values you have inherited and the stories you tell? Into what actions do they translate if they are to make a future possible?

Try this

Picture your spine, all the vertebrae. Label them with the values that keep you upright.

It is often said that "it takes a village to raise a child." Think of one particular child of whose village you are a part. Commit to one concrete thing that you can do so that this child has a childhood. Commit to one concrete thing that you can do so that this child can have a future. Commit to one concrete thing you can do to strengthen this child's spine with your values.

Dig deeper

Marilynne Robinson. *Gilead: A Novel*. Farrar, Straus & Giroux, 2004.

Anne Frank. *The Diary of a Young Girl*. Translated by Susan Massotty. Penguin Classics, 2019.

Judith Kerr. *When Hitler Stole Pink Rabbit*. Puffin Books, 2009.

Astrid Lindgren. *Mio's Kingdom*. Translated by Jill Morgan. Oxford University Press, 2003.

20
"Many Members," *or* Value Different Gifts

Reflect

Where do you see suspicion and division at work over how one should respond to the present moment? What is the result? What would it take to work in solidarity?

Have you ever seen a collaboration between genuinely different approaches or convictions? How did it come about? What did it produce?

What are your own gifts? What skills and knowledge, resources and connections, social location and access, energy and level of risk are you able to contribute to any division of labor? What do you feel unable to offer? Who do you know that can offer what you can't?

Try this

Identify one concrete skill, resource, or capacity that you have to offer, and one concrete place where you can put it to work.

Dig deeper

Sharon Welch. *After Empire: The Art and Ethos of Enduring Peace*. Fortress, 2004.

Kwok Pui-lan and Georg Rieger. *Occupy Religion: Theology of the Multitude*. Rowman & Littlefield, 2012.

adrienne maree brown. *We Will Not Cancel Us: And Other Dreams of Transformative Justice*. AK Press, 2020.

Jessica Gordon Nembhard. *Collective Courage: A History of African American Cooperative Economic Thought and Practice*. Penn State University Press, 2014.

21
"One Body," *or* Hold onto Unity

Reflect

Where do you see tendencies to uniformity? What facilitates these? What is the result?

Are there any spaces in which you meet people who are different from you, think unlike you, and yet you appreciate one another? What facilitates this? When does this become difficult?

Try this

Commit to one space that allows for disagreement and conversation between different viewpoints. What does your commitment look like, concretely?

Dig deeper

Jurjen Zeilstra. *Visser 't Hooft, 1900–1985: Living for the Unity of the Church*. Translated by Henry Jansen and Lucy Jansen-Hofland. Amsterdam University Press, 2020.

Michael Kinnamon and Brian E. Cope, eds. *The Ecumenical Movement: An Anthology of Key Texts and Voices*. Eerdmans, 1997.

Priya Parker. *The Art of Gathering: How We Meet and Why It Matters*. Riverhead Books, 2020.

adrienne maree brown. *Emergent Strategy: Shaping Change, Changing Worlds*. AK Press, 2017.

22

"Get Thee Behind Me, Satan," *or* Get out of Yourself

Reflect

What spaces are you tempted to stay in? Why? What do you appreciate about them? What do they allow you to do? Who do they allow you to be?

How can you carry those blessings forward? How can the gifts you have received turn into gifts you have to offer?

What are you receiving in solitude that the community needs? What are you receiving in the safety of your community that the world needs? What, in your opinion, would be a healthy rhythm for such a movement?

Try this

Invite someone whom you trust, or who you think might need it, into a space of safety with you.

In one space of discomfort, take an action to create comfort for others who might feel uncomfortable.

Dig deeper

Dietrich Bonhoeffer. *Discipleship*. Edited by Geffrey B. Kelly and John D. Godsey. Translated by Barbara Green and Reinhard Krauss. DBW 4. Fortress, 2015.

Audre Lorde. *Your Silence Will Not Protect You*. Silver Press, 2017.

Angela Davis. *Freedom Is a Constant Struggle: Ferguson, Palestine, and the Foundations of a Movement*. Haymarket Books, 2016.

23
"Find Power in Weakness," *or* Practice Creative Nonconformity

Reflect

Where do you see forms of compromise that attempt to avoid attention or punishment? Where do you see forms of compromise that function to humiliate and disempower those who conform?

Where do you see people refusing to conform and compromise? What are the results, and the costs? How do you feel about these examples, and why?

Discuss: Is it more important to preserve one's integrity or to preserve one's existence? Why? When do the costs for one or the other become unbearable? Do you think this is a fair alternative? What do you make of it?

Pay attention to practices of creative nonconformity around you. How do they work? What effect do they have? How do you feel about these examples, and why?

Try this

Play a "notice and name the norm" game. Throughout a day, jot down every time you feel compelled to "act normal." At the end of the day, name the norms. Ask yourself: Who benefits from these norms? Who is harmed? Track patterns.

It is easier to say yes than to say no. So name the norms that demand your yes and that demand your no to conformity. Justice? Integrity? Truth? Freedom? Empathy? In front of a mirror, practice your yes and no. Say, "I am not here to please, I am here to be true." "I am not here to be liked, I am here to love the stranger." Fill in your own yesses and nos.

Find a creative way to nonconform in an area of your choice.

Dig deeper

Václav Havel. *The Power of the Powerless: Citizens Against the State in Central-Eastern Europe*. Hutchinson, 1985.

Avishai Margalit. *On Compromise and Rotten Compromises*. Princeton University Press, 2009.

Milton Mayer. *They Thought They Were Free: The Germans 1933–45*. University of Chicago Press, 1966.

Eric L. Muller. *Lawyer, Jailer, Ally, Foe: Complicity and Conscience in America's World War II Concentration Camps*. University of North Carolina Press, 2023.

Max H. Bazerman and Ann E. Tenbrunsel. *Blind Spots: Why We Fail to Do What's Right and What to Do About It*. Princeton University Press, 2013.

Erich Fromm. *On Disobedience: Why Freedom Means Saying "No" to Power*. Harper Perennial, 2019.

24

"Prepare the Ground," *or* Cultivate Relationships

Reflect

Think of a person who has been a long-standing mentor or friend to you. How has your relationship grown, changed, and been sustained through time? What have you invested to keep it alive? What are you currently doing to nourish it?

Think of one dear relationship that has withered. How and why has this happened? Was it due to disappointment or estrangement, a falling out or a growing apart? Could there have been a different end? Why or why not?

Think of one relationship where you feel your trust was misplaced, your efforts mis-invested. How and why? In hindsight, were there any signs you could have spotted? If you had known early, would you have behaved differently? Why or why not?

Try this

Think of three people you trust but are not frequently in touch with. Reach out and reconnect.

Think of one person who is very close to you and resolve to share four things (thoughts, concerns, feelings, etc.) with them over the coming four days.

Think of one person who is quite close to you and resolve to share four things (meals, walks, conversations, etc.) with them over the coming four weeks.

Think of one person who is far away and resolve to share four things (phone calls, visits, parcels, etc.) with them over the coming four months.

Dig deeper

Paulo Freire. *Pedagogy of the Oppressed*. Translated by Myra Bergman Ramos. Fiftieth anniversary ed. Bloomsbury Academic, 2017.

bell hooks. *Teaching Community: A Pedagogy of Hope*. Routledge, 2003.

Jeffrey Stout. *Blessed Are the Organized: Grassroots Democracy in America*. Princeton University Press, 2012.

Marshall Ganz. *People, Power, Change: Organizing for Democratic Renewal*. Oxford University Press, 2024.

Raimundo C. Barreto. *Base Ecumenism: Latin American Contributions to Ecumenical Praxis and Theology*. Fortress, 2025.

25
"Love Your Neighbor," *or* Shatter Loneliness

Reflect

Do you know your neighbors? The person living next to you, your coworker, the clerk at the store, the crossing guard on your street, the secretary at your school—do you know their name?

Would you become aware if something changed in their life? Would you notice if they withdrew or disappeared? Would you notice if they were frightened or if they became radicalized? How would you spot the signs?

Try this

Make it a standing practice to establish eye contact with and greet the people you share physical space with.

Strike up a conversation with a person with whom you share space but maybe not much else. Ask them how they are doing, ask them two follow-up questions. Repeat the next time you see them.

Think of one particular neighbor. What is one concrete way that you can provide everyday assistance to them?

Dig deeper

Hannah Arendt. *The Origins of Totalitarianism*. Penguin, 2017.

Dietrich Bonhoeffer. *Life Together*. Translated by Daniel W. Bloesch. DBW 5. Fortress, 2015.

Karl Barth. *Church Dogmatics* I/2. *The Life of the Children of God: The Praise of God*, 404–56. Translated by G. W. Bromiley. T&T Clark, 1957.

Nancy L. Rosenblum. *Good Neighbors: The Democracy of Everyday Life in America*. Princeton University Press, 2016.

Jane Jacobs. *The Death and Life of Great American Cities*. Random House, 1961.

Dean Spade. *Mutual Aid: Building Solidarity During This Crisis (and the Next)*. Verso, 2020.

26
"Redeem the Time," *or* Delay and Prepare

Reflect

Where and how can you use time for your benefit and the benefit of those you care about?

What are threats and developments you anticipate, and how can you prepare for them effectively? What measures can you put into place to keep yourself and those you care about alive, functional, and supported under various scenarios?

Where is time working against you and those you care about? What can you do about this?

Try this

Set up powers of attorney and a living will. Apply for a passport.

Set up automatic bill payments. Make sure your car and other important hardware are in good shape.

Have a stock of medications and provisions you regularly need.

Make lists of important contacts and passwords. Have cash on hand and an emergency plan in place.

Dig deeper

David M. Crowe. *Oskar Schindler: The Untold Account of His Life, Wartime Activities, and the True Story Behind the List.* Westview, 2004.

Bo Lidegaard. *Countrymen: The Untold Story of How Denmark's Jews Escaped the Nazis, of the Courage of Their Fellow Danes—and of the Extraordinary Role of the SS*. Knopf, 2013.

Ludivine Broch. *Ordinary Workers, Vichy, and the Holocaust: French Railwaymen and the Second World War*. Cambridge University Press, 2016.

Ulrich Alexander Boschwitz. *The Passenger*. Translated by Philip Boehm. Metropolitan Books, 2021.

27
"Come to Me . . . ," *or* Allow People to Change

Reflect

Have you ever changed your mind on a significant issue? What prompted it? What made the change easier? What made it difficult?

What might be the signs of a person who wants to change? How would you spot them?

Is it possible to hold a person accountable without shaming or blaming them? How, and how not? What might be ways to do that?

Try this

Write down the name of one friend, relative, or neighbor who might have doubts about the political direction of this country. What will you do to make space for their doubts?

Dig deeper

Miroslav Volf. *The End of Memory: Remembering Rightly in a Violent World*. Eerdmans, 2006.

Susan Neiman. *Learning from the Germans: Race and the Memory of Evil*. Farrar, Straus & Giroux, 2019.

Coline Covington. *Who's to Blame? Collective Guilt on Trial.* Routledge, 2023.

Howard Zehr. *Changing Lenses: Restorative Justice for Our Times*. Herald, 2015.

Ta-Nehisi Coates. "The Case for Reparations." *Atlantic*, June 2014. https://tinyurl.com/3b5ddc2m.

28

"What Do You Have That You Did Not Receive?," or Pass on the Word

Reflect

What are your go-to sources for insight and wisdom? Why these?

Have you ever found insight in unexpected places? Where and how? What came of it?

How will your own insights survive? How will your experiences help other people, in other times and places, that you might not even know personally, or ever meet?

Try this

Pick a historical or cultural context, an artistic or spiritual tradition, a movement or institution you are interested in and learn more about it.

Identify a partnership your community already has and leverage it for mutual learning. This may be a similar community in another place or another organization in the same place, an ecumenical network or interfaith organization. What can you do to strengthen communication, exchange, and sharing of wisdom?

Dig deeper

Rowan Williams. *Why Study the Past? The Quest for the Historical Church*. Eerdmans, 2005.

Jaroslav Pelikan. *The Vindication of Tradition: The 1983 Jefferson Lecture in the Humanities*. Yale University Press, 1984.

Matt Jenson. *Theology in the Democracy of the Dead: A Dialogue with the Living Tradition*. Baker Academic, 2019.

Sharon Welch. *Communities of Resistance and Solidarity: A Feminist Theology of Liberation*. Wipf & Stock, 2017.

Yolanda Pierce. *In My Grandmother's House: Black Women, Faith, and the Stories We Inherit*. Broadleaf Books, 2021.

Conclusion
"Build Houses . . . ," *or* Transform Your Hope

Reflect

Take inventory of the things you see dying. Which of these do you mourn and why? To which are you saying "good riddance," and why?

Which hopes might we have to give up? What do you think will be left? What do you want to do with it?

There is much to fear. But what concrete hopes do you have for the time to come? What forms might your love and your faith, your commitments and beliefs, take on?

Try this

Renounce one hope that no longer fits. Name it, grieve it, bury it.

Read a book or watch a movie about a time that is long gone.

Plant a tree.

Dig deeper

Steven Levitsky and Daniel Ziblatt. *How Democracies Die*. Crown, 2019.

Peter Heather and John Rapley. *Why Empires Fall: Rome, America, and the Future of the West*. Yale University Press, 2023.

Franz Werfel. *Hearken unto the Voice*. Viking, 1938.

Ted A. Smith. *The End of Theological Education*. Eerdmans, 2023.

James K. A. Smith. *How to Inhabit Time: Understanding the Past, Facing the Future, Living Faithfully Now*. Brazos, 2022.

Acknowledgments

In late 2024, Yanan Melo invited me to give a talk, "Doing Theology in a Time of War," for a cohort of young leaders he was convening within Amar Peterman's Good Road Network. At the time, the war foremost on our mind was probably the Israel Defense Forces' unrelenting, US-funded annihilating onslaught on Gaza after Hamas's horrendous attack of October 7, 2023. Even so, the ongoing brutality in Syria, Sudan, Congo, and Myanmar, Russia's aggression against Ukraine and fears about its ramifications for Europe and NATO, planetary catastrophes and streams of climate refugees, increasing geopolitical tensions over resources and access between states, and spiraling polarization at home all fed into the sense that we were living in "a time of war" of which individual conflicts were but symptoms.

Then, Donald Trump took office. At what his advisor Steve Bannon called "muzzle velocity," Trump unleashed a stream of executive orders that laid waste to federal institutions, democratic culture, and international relations. He effectively declared war on immigrants and trans people, on free speech and higher education. He waged tariff wars and spewed threats against neighboring states and long-standing allies.

By the time I was to give my talk, I found myself wondering: How could I speak about a "time of war" somewhere *out there* as if I was not struggling to come up with wisdom for the tumult right here, right now? And what did I have to offer? As I was reeling from the news every day, historical voices popped into my head. Rather than attempting to say *something*, myself, I slowed down to listen to them, reflect on them, and let them speak to me.

Writing these meditations became a kind of spiritual discipline for me. It helped me process political developments in real time that would otherwise have overwhelmed me, and reoriented me to my beliefs, commitments, and values. It created a space for self-examination and gave my response a ground that was not just a place of anxiety. All I can hope is that they might be able to do something similar for others.

A recurrent theme in these meditations is friendship and community. They are not just instrumental to the pursuit of a different world; they are its reality in the midst of this one. As I started sharing bits and pieces, colleagues, students, neighbors responded with their own perspective, wisdom, and concerns. Individual conversations often inspired entire new pieces. Eventually they coalesced into this small book.

I am so grateful: To Brandy Daniels and Keri Day for many invigorating cowriting conspirations, to William Stell for always sharing joys and concerns on the run, to Heath Carter for his unrelenting combative optimism over serious beers. To Brandy Daniels, Samuel Davidson, Frederike van Oorschot, Emily Pruszinski, Jürgen Reichel, Rosa Ross, and Joachim Vette for comprehensive and thoughtful feedback. To Yanan Melo, Amar Peterman, Wendy Cordero Rugama, and Annah Kuriakose for workshopping the manuscript in their cohort after my initial talk, greatly improving content, structure, and style. To Eric Barreto, John Bowlin, Denise Carrell, K. C. Choi, Julia Enxing, Benedikt Friedrich-Lang, Isanthe Heberger-Demel, Elaine James, Melissa Martin, Erin Raffety, Thomas Renkert, Beth Scibienski, Lindsey Scott, Dirk Smit, Sarah Stewart-Kroeker, Mark Taylor, Kim Wagner, and Michael Welker for encouragement, rebukes, inspiration, and conspiration—whether on walks around the block or in textual exchanges halfway around the globe. To Emily Pruszinski for thorough support with editing, citations, and getting the manuscript into shape.

I am deeply indebted to Eerdmans Publishing: to Lisa Ann Cockrel, who immediately affirmed that this project should be a book and accompanied it so wonderfully through the whole process, to James Ernest for affirmation and exhortation, to Jenny Hoffman for project management, to Jeff Dundas, Jason Pearson, William Bergkamp, Claire McColley, and Clare Galloway for publicity and marketing, to Heather Brewer for the wonderful cover design, to Laurel Draper for assistance with corrections, and to the whole team for the special commitment and labor it meant to get it into print in such a timely and professional manner.

A research fellowship at the Protestantse Theologische Universiteit in Utrecht, and the hospitality of the Evangelische Broedergemeente Zeist afforded me the space and time to complete the manuscript in March 2025 during a sabbatical from Princeton Theological Seminary. Many good people made this stay a treat: Heleen Zorgdrager and Arnold Huijgen stand out among them. None of it would have been possible without the support of Ulrike Bornecke-Menacher.

Above all, I thank Moritz Menacher for his quiet, courageous, and steadfast partnership regardless of how restless or anxious I become.

Notes

Chapter 1

1. Dietrich Bonhoeffer, *Letters and Papers from Prison*, ed. John W. de Gruchy, trans. Isabel Best et al., Dietrich Bonhoeffer Works 8 (Fortress, 2010), 404–5. Dietrich Bonhoeffer Works hereafter abbreviated DBW.

2. Karl Barth, *Church Dogmatics* III/3 (T&T Clark, 1960), 523.

3. Karl Barth, *Theological Existence To-Day: A Plea for Theological Freedom*, trans. R. Birch Hoyle (Wipf & Stock, 2012), 9.

4. Karl Barth to Joseph Hromádka, September 19, 1938, cited in Eberhard Busch, *Karl Barth: His Life from Letters and Autobiographical Texts* (Wipf & Stock, 2005), 289.

Chapter 1

1. The serenity prayer quickly started circulating widely in several variations, often without attribution to Niebuhr, up to becoming a standard mantra of Alcoholics Anonymous.

Niebuhr himself used different wordings on different occasions, both orally and in print.

2. León Gieco, "Solo le pido a Dios," *4°LP* (Orfeon Videovox, 1978). Lyrics used with permission of León Gieco, Argentina, translation mine.

3. Viktor E. Frankl, *Man's Search for Meaning* (Beacon, 2006), part 1.

Chapter 3

1. Karl Barth, *The Epistle to the Romans*, trans. Edwyn C. Hoskyns (Oxford University Press, 1968), 483.

Chapter 4

1. Karl Barth, *Dogmatics in Outline* (Harper & Row, 1959), 48.

2. Harry G. Frankfurt, *On Bullshit* (Princeton University Press, 2005).

Chapter 5

1. Stuttgart Declaration of Guilt (October 18, 1945), in Matthew D. Hockenos, *A Church Divided: German Protestants Confront the Nazi Past* (Indiana University Press, 2004), 187.

2. Darmstadt Statement (August 1947), in Hockenos, *A Church Divided*, 193.

3. Darmstadt Statement, 194.

4. Bonhoeffer, *Letters and Papers from Prison*, 46.

Chapter 6

1. Frankl, *Man's Search for Meaning*.

Chapter 7

1. The Barmen Declaration, in *The Book of Confessions of the PC (USA)*, 8.11 (hereafter cited as *BoC*).

2. The Heidelberg Catechism, Q&A 1, in *BoC* 4.001.

3. The Barmen Declaration, in *BoC* 8.14, 8.21.

Chapter 8

1. Gregory H. Stanton, "The Ten Stages of Genocide," Genocide Watch, 1996, https://tinyurl.com/t2rwxk95.

2. Martin Luther, *Heidelberg Disputation*, Q21, https://tinyurl.com/3uahtep2.

3. Dietrich Bonhoeffer, "What Is Meant by 'Telling the Truth'?" in *Conspiracy and Imprisonment, 1940–1945*, ed. Mark S. Brocker, trans. Lisa E. Dahill, DBW 16 (Fortress, 2006), 622.

4. Victor Klemperer, *The Language of the Third Reich*, trans. Martin Brady (Bloomsbury Academic, 2013).

5. George Orwell, *Nineteen Eighty-Four* (Buccaneer, 1949).

6. Ray Bradbury, *Fahrenheit 451* (Simon & Schuster, 2012).

Chapter 9

1. Bonhoeffer, "Christen und Heiden," in *Widerstand und Ergebung: Briefe und Aufzeichnungen aus der Haft*, ed. Christian Gremmels et al., DBW 8 (Gütersloher Verlagshaus, 1998), 515–16, translation by Martin Tel and me.

2. Belhar Confession, in *BoC* 10.7.

3. Dietrich Bonhoeffer, "Texts from University Lectures: Summer Semester 1932," in *Ecumenical, Academic, and Pastoral Work: 1931–1932*, ed. Victoria J. Barnett, Mark S. Brocker,

and Michael B. Lukens, trans. Anne Schmidt-Lange et al., DBW 11 (Fortress, 2012), 296–97.

Chapter 10

1. Mariann Edgar Budde, "'Contempt Is a Dangerous Way to Lead a Country': Here Is the Sermon That Enraged Donald Trump," *Guardian*, January 24, 2025, https://tinyurl.com/yax36m8w.

2. Ashleigh Fields, "GOP Member Wants Bishop 'Added to Deportation List' After Trump Prayer Service," *Hill*, January 21, 2025, https://tinyurl.com/yf2mp27t.

3. Martin Niemöller used slightly different versions of this confessional poem on different occasions. This is the version of the Holocaust Memorial Day Trust, https://tinyurl.com/3v8apxkm.

Chapter 11

1. Bonhoeffer, *Letters and Papers from Prison*, 233.

Chapter 12

1. Timothy Snyder, *On Tyranny: Twenty Lessons from the Twentieth Century* (Crown, 2017), 17.

2. Barmen Declaration, Thesis I (*BoC* 8.11), Thesis II (*BoC* 8.15).

Chapter 14

1. Timothy George, "Something Bold for God: Huldrych Zwingli," in *Theology of the Reformers* (Broadman & Holman, 2013), 165. Original source, *Huldreich Zwinglis Samtliche*

Werke, ed. Emil Egli, Georg Finsler, et al. (Berlin, Leipzig, Zürich, 1950), 10:165.

2. Sophie Scholl in court before judge Roland Freisler on February 22, 1943, cited in Richard Hanser, *A Noble Treason: The Story of Sophie Scholl and the White Rose Revolt Against Hitler vs the Revolt of the Munich Students Against Hitler* (Ignatius, 2012), 18.

3. While widely circulated and often credited to Sophie Scholl directly, the quote is from Lillian Garrett-Groag's play, *The White Rose* (Dramatists Play Service, 1993), 62.

4. Carlo Mierendorf, "Die volle Wahrheit," *Sozialistische Monatshefte* 38, no. 5 (1932): 297–304, popularized by Paul F. Lazarsfeld, Bernard Berelson, and Hazel Gaudet, *The People's Choice: How the Voter Makes Up His Mind in a Presidential Campaign* (Columbia University Press, 2021).

5. Hannah Arendt, *The Life of the Mind* (Harcourt, 1978), 180.

Chapter 15

1. Cf. chapter 2.

2. Westminster Shorter Catechism, 1A, *BoC* 7.001.

3. *Etty: The Letters and Diaries of Etty Hillesum, 1941–1943, Complete and Unabridged*, ed. Klaas A. D. Smelik, trans. Arnold J. Pomerans (Eerdmans, 2002), 545.

4. Smelik, *Etty*, 489.

5. Smelik, *Etty*, 658.

6. Smelik, *Etty*, 305.

7. Smelik, *Etty*, 488, 536.

8. Patrick Woodhouse, *Etty Hillesum: A Life Transformed* (Bloomsbury, 2009), 136.

Chapter 16

1. A virtual private network (VPN) protects your identity and activity online from prying eyes. It encrypts internet traffic and routes it through your VPN provider's server before connecting to websites or other internet services.

2. Dietrich Bonhoeffer, *Life Together*, ed. Geffrey B. Kelly, trans. Daniel W. Bloesch and James H. Burtness, DBW 5 (Fortress, 1996), 82.

Chapter 17

1. Bonhoeffer, *Life Together*, 29.

2. Bonhoeffer, *Life Together*, 35.

Chapter 18

1. Johann Baptist Metz, "'Politische Theologie' in der Diskussion (1969)," in *Neue Politische Theologie: Versuch eines Korrektivs der Theologie*, ed. Johann Reikerstorfer, Gesammelte Schriften 3/2 (Herder, 2016), 46, translation mine.

2. Theodor Adorno, "Education After Auschwitz," in *Critical Models: Interventions and Catchwords*, trans. Henry Pickford (Columbia University Press, 2005), 191.

3. Susannah Heschel, "Meir Kahane and Race as Incarnational Theology," *Journal of Religious Ethics* 50, no. 2 (June 2022): 300.

Chapter 19

1. Bonhoeffer, "After Ten Years," in *Letters and Papers from Prison*, 42.

2. Astrid Lindgren, *The Brothers Lionheart*, illustrated by Ilon Wickland, trans. Jill Morgan (Purple House Press, 2004), 164.

Chapter 21

1. Willem A. Visser 't Hooft, "The Calling of the World Council of Churches," *Ecumenical Review* 14, no. 2 (1962): 224.

2. Michael Kinnamon, *Unity as a Prophetic Witness: W. A. Visser 't Hooft and the Shaping of Ecumenical Theology* (Fortress, 2018), 29.

Chapter 23

1. Václav Havel, *The Power of the Powerless: Citizens Against the State in Central-Eastern Europe*, trans. John Keane (Hutchinson, 1985), 9, 7.

2. Havel, *Power of the Powerless*, 9.

Chapter 25

1. Derek Thompson, "The Anti-Social Century," *Atlantic*, January 8, 2025, https://tinyurl.com/3y62zrca.

2. Bonhoeffer, *Life Together*, 32.

Chapter 26

1. Bonhoeffer to Bethge, November 18, 1943, in *Letters and Papers from Prison*, 180.

Chapter 27

1. Karl Barth, "Die Deutschen und Wir," in *Eine Schweizer Stimme 1938–1945* (Evangelischer Verlag, 1945), 354–55, translation mine.

Conclusion

1. Edward Gibbon's monumental history covers the period from 98 CE to 1590 CE. Cf. Edward Gibbon, *The History of the Decline and Fall of the Roman Empire*, 6 vols. (Strahan & Cadell, 1776–1789).

2. Ted Smith, *The End of Theological Education* (Eerdmans, 2023).

3. According to Jane E. Strohl, this widely cited saying of his is unverified. See Jane E. Strohl, "Luther's Spiritual Journey," in *The Cambridge Companion to Martin Luther*, ed. Donald K. McKim (Cambridge University Press, 2003), 162.